INTERNATIONAL
CONFLICT
for
beginners

INTERNATIONAL

HARPER TORCHBOOKS
Harper & Row, Publishers
New York, Hagerstown, San Francisco, London

CONFLICT

for beginners

by Roger Fisher

Illustrations by Robert C. Osborn

INTERNATIONAL CONFLICT FOR BEGINNERS. *Copyright* © *1969 by Roger Fisher. Illustrations copyright* © *1969 by Harper & Row, Publishers, Incorporated. Printed in the United States of America. All rights reserved. No part of this book may be used or reproduced in any manner whatsoever without written permission except in the case of brief quotations embodied in critical articles and reviews. For information address Harper & Row, Publishers, Inc., 10 East 53rd Street, New York, N.Y. 10022. Published simultaneously in Canada by Fitzhenry & Whiteside Limited, Toronto.*

LIBRARY OF CONGRESS CATALOG CARD NUMBER: 69-17292

ISBN: 0-06-131911-2

82 83 84   20 19 18 17 16 15 14 13 12

To

John McNaughton
1921–1967

Who never hesitated to ask what
the emperor was wearing or otherwise to inject common sense into
the conduct of international affairs.

CONTENTS

Acknowledgment

THE ideas in this book have grown over such a period of time, and have gone through such transformations, that it is impossible for me to give appropriate thanks to all those who have contributed to them. To friends, colleagues and students, I owe more than gratitude.

I must, however, mention at least those who might well have appeared on the title page as co-authors. During the academic year 1964–1965 I worked with a Freshman Seminar in Harvard College on the problem of controlling the magnitude of issues in international conflict. The analytic approach used in this book was developed in that seminar and was first written up in a working draft called *What's the Message?—An Approach to International Conflict* of which the authors were the seminar members: Martha-Ann Ackelsberg, Don Berwick, Bill Blumberg, Bill Bullitt, Jackie Evans, Stuart Fuchs, Bill Kelly, Sherry Leeright, Kevin Mellyn, Peter Petri, Steve Presser, Debbie Slotkin, Tim Wilton and myself. We had a good time in the seminar and I, at least, learned a lot. In case the extent of my pleasure in their company camouflaged the extent of my indebtedness to them, let me record it here.

The following year I spent visiting the International Relations Department at the London School of Economics as a Guggenheim Fellow and writing a draft of what later turned into this book. I am grateful to the John Simon Guggenheim Memorial Foundation and to the London School of Economics for the opportunity to work among such stimulating and pleasant colleagues.

At the London School of Economics I met George Frampton, Jr., who during the succeeding year at Harvard Law School, worked with me so closely in taking that draft apart and putting this book together that neither of us can be sure which words are whose. His contribution not only to this book but also to my enjoyment in working on it is beyond measure.

No reader can miss what Robert Osborn has done for this book. With his drawings he has unquestionably won our long-standing debate over the comparative merits of artists' lines and lawyers' words.

Foreword

THIS is a small but potent book. It is a product of today that hopefully will help shape many tomorrows.

In form it is disarmingly simple—a handbook for officials in government and others who are interested in international affairs. In a straightforward way, it presents some organized common sense about the conduct of these affairs, amply illustrated by discussion on such current problems as Vietnam, Korea, Cuba, Rhodesia and the Middle East.

The book suggests that the essential strategy for exerting influence upon other governments is to change the questions at issue. It is important, therefore, that in dealing with others, we seek to understand how they view a problem, and make every effort to alter their perception. Moreover, when others make what we regard as mistakes, we should respond by opening up to them new choices, rather than simply threatening dire political, economic or military consequences for their actions.

The unique power of this book lies in the fact that Roger Fisher is practicing on his readers the very strategy he is preaching. He is engaged in changing our perception of international affairs and in opening up new choices in how we approach the multitude of problems in building a better world, so that we can avoid repeating some errors of the past.

Rather than asking more about the complexities of every dispute, this book asks about their basic essentials. Rather than asking about the past, it asks about the future—and here it does not ask what we are probably going to do, but what we ought to do. Rather than asking first about *our* options, it suggests that we ask first about the options of those we are trying to influence. Rather than directing our attention to the factors which limit our freedom, it directs our attention to the wise exercise of the freedom that we have. Rather than bemoaning the irrational forces which affect so much of what happens in the world, it challenges us to use our forces rationally to affect what we can.

When we look back and ask "Why?" we look for cause and explanations of why what happened was inevitable. When we look forward and ask "Why?" we look for purpose, and we look for means well-designed to achieve that purpose. The more we apply ourselves to that task the greater our chance to affect the future.

Robert Kennedy once wrote:

Our future may lie beyond our vision, but it is not completely beyond our control. It is the shaping impulse of America that neither fate nor nature nor the irresistible tides of history, but the work of our own hands, matched to reason and principle, will determine destiny.

Roger Fisher reflects this impulse. This book makes it a little more likely that reason and principle will determine the future course of international events.

EDWARD M. KENNEDY

Introduction

IN form this book is a how-to-do-it guide for statesmen—a primer on the conduct of that limited portion of international affairs concerned with immediate conflicts. I chose this form for several reasons. First, it directs attention toward basics, toward some of the simple, first principles which should guide the conduct of conflict. Before we disagree about the accuracy of the latest trade figures from Southern Rhodesia or the number of planes needed in Thailand, I believe we should back off and look at some of the big questions about what we are trying to do and how we propose to do it. The concept of a primer, or handbook, lets me suggest without embarrassment a simple framework for thinking. After some twenty years of being professionally concerned with international affairs I find such a framework useful. I hope others will.

Secondly, this approach sharpens facts by confronting them with the cutting edge of choice. I am often told that

I spend my time prescribing what decision-makers ought to do while true social science is concerned with what decision-makers actually do. I flatly reject this view that it is more scientific to adopt the vantage point of a pure spectator rather than of a potential actor. For a pure spectator there are no criteria of relevance. On the other hand, trying to answer the question of what ought to be done requires a more perceptive eye on what actually happens than does a factual description of foreign affairs. Adopting the vantage point of an adviser to a statesman engaged in the conduct of international affairs excludes nothing. An adviser is as interested in the actual world of foreign affairs as any social science researcher. To advise a statesman as to how he ought to behave, one needs to know all there is to be known about how other statesmen really behave, about cause and effect, and about the predictable consequences of various courses of action. The handbook form excludes nothing, I believe, but rather tries to marshal the facts in a more useful fashion. This is not to say that I have succeeded, but only to justify the attempt.

A third advantage of the handbook form is that it directs attention to the *conduct* of foreign affairs rather than to something called "policy." The very concept of foreign policy suggests that the important question to ask is, "What is our policy?" It promotes the belief that the central task of people in the State Department and in other ministries of foreign affairs is to produce a generalized statement of a posture or position which can be maintained over a period of time. A how-to-do-it approach emphasizes that there are things to do as well as policies to produce. It makes it easier to talk about the skills of conflict management and the skills of communicating with governments with whom we differ.

One disadvantage of putting ideas in the form of advice

is that the client or reader may get the impression that I think the ideas will "work" in some objective sense. This book is not intended to solve problems, but to identify them, and to suggest an approach. A gardening book will not make plants grow in the face of a drought; a sailing guide will not guide a boat through every storm nor help it win every race; nor will a book on how to shop for antiques bridge the gap between lofty objectives and limited resources. A book on how to influence another government is no exception. Often the only reconciliation between objectives and resources is to lower one's sights. If a how-to-do-it book means that it can be done this is really a how-to-go-about-it book.

Perhaps the primary advantage of the present format is that it may be provocative. Advice and conclusions are more quickly challenged than a theoretical description. Most of my theories and assumptions are not subject to proof, but neither are the assumptions upon which governments currently operate. We will have to battle them out and in this process the more controversy the better. Some of this controversy may be over the format itself. I have already been told by one friend in the government, "Your approach is much too abstract, and besides I now do what you suggest every day."

INTERNATIONAL
CONFLICT
for
beginners

1

Think First About Their Decision

JUDGED by any standard the international situation is in a mess. It is destructive and dangerous and likely to become more so. But if the international situation is in a mess, it is not because governments are incapable of doing what they think they ought to be doing. It is because governments too often conceive of foreign affairs in ways which make their actions ineffective and conflict-prone. Governments too often regard their task as that of adopting a morally and politically justifiable posture or attitude rather than that of obtaining the best results that can be obtained under the circumstances.

The central task of foreign affairs is to make choices about what a government says or does in the international field. Other activities, like information gathering and predicting, are incidental and should be organized to reflect the purpose for which the information is being gathered and the purpose for which the prediction is being made.

The collecting of facts cannot be the end of foreign policy. There are an infinite number of facts about the world. Among these truths there is no objective criterion of importance. Information is useless except as it is used. One set of facts about an international situation can be said to be better than another only when we identify both the person for whom it is better and the purpose for which it is better. Gathering facts without regard to the purpose for which they are being gathered is likely to direct attention to "hard" facts that are certain and to divert attention from matters that are less certain but more important.

Predicting the future without regard to the way in which that prediction is to be used is an even less useful and more hazardous activity. To concentrate attention on matters we can predict is to give less attention to matters we can affect. Further, predictions about foreign affairs usually involve some element of what we ourselves are going to do. Such predictions tend to blur rather than to sharpen the capacity for clear thinking. A prediction that my family will go on a picnic next Sunday, for example, is in part a prediction of the weather and of other factors completely beyond my control. In part it is a prediction of what other members of the family will do. But it is not useful in helping us to decide whether or not to go on a picnic. The prediction is not a discussion of the reasons for going and for not going, nor does it identify promising alternatives to a picnic. It is not even a discussion of alternative picnic spots. Finally, my prediction is, in part, a prediction of what I myself am going to do. This means looking at my future choice in terms of what I am most likely to do, not in terms of what I ought to do. And any prediction I make about my own behavior has a tendency to become self-fulfilling; doing what I predicted I would do avoids the necessity of any further thought about the matter and also proves the accuracy of my prediction.

Information gathering and predicting are clearly subordinate functions to the job of making choices about what the government should do in the international field. That task is usually identified as "decision making," in which the focus, both initially and finally, is on the decision which we, the government, make, or ought to make. Certainly, the final question is properly what do we do. But to take that as the initial question obscures the crucial relationship between our actions and what we are trying to accomplish.

In essence, foreign affairs are affairs which take place outside the United States. They are thus affairs which are not under the exclusive control of the United States but ones in which all or a substantial part of the action is being taken by or with the acquiescence of a foreign government. If we start with the question of what *we* should do or say about some such matter, we tend to adopt a posture of response: What should our attitude be toward what is going on? For the State Department, the result of a decision is usually words—a policy statement, a speech at the United Nations, a diplomatic protest, a position paper, a cable, or a press release. The Department sees its task not as producing results but rather as producing something called "policy." The State Department often behaves as if its sole function were to produce attitudes and platitudes.

We would not think much of a doctor who, instead of dealing with actual patients and diseases, saw his function as that of announcing a proper attitude toward them. If confronted with a case of smallpox, such a doctor would

categorically announce that he was opposed to smallpox.
When faced with cases of measles or mumps, our policy-
oriented doctor would adopt a balanced attitude, pointing
out that while he was not opposed to such diseases in pre-
adolescent children, we should not underestimate their risks
for adults. It is not unfair to suggest that too large a part
of foreign policy making is producing words which simply
define a posture or attitude.

It is worse than that. Foreign policy making is seen as
producing an attitude that is not merely appropriate for a
particular situation; the objective is to produce an all-purpose attitude which will serve for many different situations
over a long period of time. Consistency is deemed a great
virtue of foreign policy. A statement of our position is
deemed better the more often it has been said before. By
the time an attitude has been stated and restated by four
Presidents—by the time it has become a platitude—it has
become a firmly entrenched bit of United States foreign
policy. And by that time it may be worse than useless. Whatever merit there may have been in the posture when first
adopted, little good is accomplished by repeating slogans
such as "no appeasement," "open covenants openly arrived
at," "we must honor our commitments," and "we are in favor
of the United Nations." Such maxims take on a life of their
own and become substitutes for thought. The conduct of
foreign affairs is seen less as the exercise of a governmental
skill and more as the articulation of an all-purpose answer.

Part of the fault may lie in the very word "policy." We
ask the State Department what our foreign policy is toward
Greece, but we do not ask the Post Office Department what
its policy is toward Iowa, or the Defense Department what
its policy is toward guns. The proper answer to the latter
questions would presumably be that the policy is to be wise,

It is with a feeling, for us, of regret & concern,
that we view the most recent regressive
encroachment of territorial waters by...etc.etc.

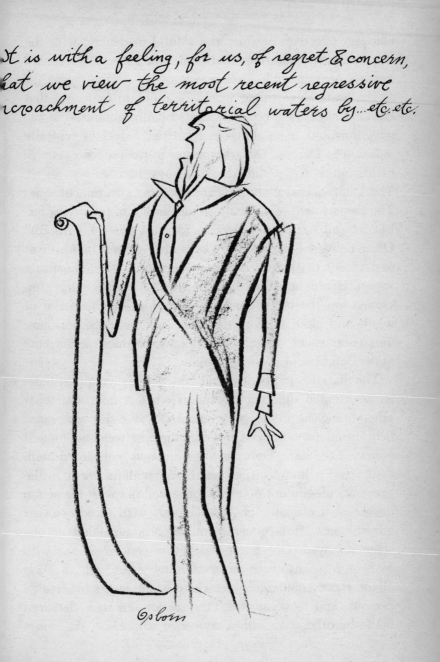

Osbert

efficient, effective, flexible, and skillful in dealing with the many different questions that come up. Perhaps we should look for a comparable foreign policy.

The State Department would be quick to point out that the kind of decision typically made by other branches of the government is quite different from that which it typically makes. The Defense Department moves troops, orders equipment, builds bases, and designs, buys, and sells weapons. The Department of the Interior operates government land. The Department of Agriculture develops and publicizes fertilizers and institutes programs for pest control. The Post Office delivers the mail. The Corps of Engineers builds dikes and levees. All of them make decisions which result in action. Decisions with which the State Department is concerned, on the other hand, are decisions in the realm of words and ideas: diplomatic notes and speeches, positions, and conferences. Other departments produce action; the State Department produces policy.

The State Department would be right in saying that there is an essential difference between what it does and what other branches of the government do. But that difference is best understood not as the difference between action and policy. The State Department is just as concerned with action and action decisions as any other department in the government—except that it is concerned not with the action decisions of our own government but with those of other governments. It is governmental decision making at one stage removed. Our foreign policy is concerned not with making decisions about our own country but with affecting all of those comparable decisions when made by foreign persons and governments: the action-oriented decisions made by others. As with a lawyer or a lobbyist, the things which the State Department ought to say and do are best understood not as "decisions" in their own right but as moves intended to influence decisions which they want others to take.

The Planned Parenthood Federation would be doing a poor job if they simply asked themselves to propound a "policy" toward the population problem. They would not do much better if they started by asking themselves what decisions they should make. Instead, they start as they should by asking themselves what decisions they want the government to make and how they should go about getting the government to make them. The essential decision for the lawyer as advocate is deciding what decision he wants the judge to make; the lawyer's task is to convince the judge to make that decision. The lobbyist starts by identifying what kind of draft bill he would like to see introduced, and which congressman he wants to introduce it, or what regulation he would like passed. The lawyer begins by identifying a cease-and-desist order which he would like the court to issue or a principle he would like the court to propound.

The central feature of foreign affairs is that its problems arise where other governments have the power to make decisions. Major actors are those whom we do not control. The resolution of international problems requires actions—decisions—by countries other than ourselves. We will, I believe, be more effective in foreign affairs if we realize that most of the job consists of exerting influence—usually marginal—on the decisions of others.

There are, of course, some international objectives which we can accomplish, some problems which we may be able to solve, which do not involve the decisions of other countries. One way for us to achieve an objective is to do it ourselves. If we cannot persuade an adversary to give us something, perhaps we can take it.

Self-help is an efficient way of accomplishing things, since it requires no decision by an adversary. But it is effective only when dealing with a physical problem, typically of a military sort, like taking Iwo Jima or knocking out a bridge. Within a country the government can often produce the result it desires by this means: towing an automobile, removing a billboard, locking up a dangerous man, or fencing a park. And to some extent one government can control what another government does in the same manner. The United States tries to prevent other governments from acquiring secret information by locking it up and by capturing their spies. The Soviet Union has from time to time physically limited the degree to which the United States may propagandize the Soviet people by jamming radio broadcasts and by restricting the inflow of publications. India, wishing to increase its share of water from the River Sutlej at the expense of Pakistan, was in an upstream position where it could simply divert the water. Through reconnaissance satellites we can help ourselves to some information. But it is surprising how few important international objectives can be achieved in this way.

"Education" is one other way of pursuing an international objective which does not require somebody else to make a decision. Part of our efforts abroad are directed toward changing the long-range values or attitudes of others; exerting this kind of influence is unrelated to any present decision which we want them to make. We want to affect not what they say or do but what they think. Foreign aid, student exchange, and the Voice of America are activities usually unrelated to any particular conflict or confrontation. They are investments in attitude, values, perceptions, or, sometimes, skills. We are concerned with their state of mind when we talk about our reputation or about demonstrating the kind of country we are. We may want others to think of us as powerful, or tough, or honest, or generous, or democratic, or rich, but there is nothing we now want them to decide to do. We want them to have certain ideas about us in the back of their mind which we may be able to draw on at some indeterminate future date.

These two ways of attaining international objectives— self-help and education—are simply not applicable to most conflict situations. Almost any conflict can be seen as an attempt by one government to influence another government to do or say something or not to do or say something. That is, a conflict is a situation in which one government wants another government to change their* mind with regard to something they have done or are threatening to do. In any conflict there is something we would like them to say or do which could avoid the crisis, limit the conflict, or settle the difference. There is some decision they could make which would avoid a clash. In most conflicts the issues which are in dispute cannot be settled or avoided either by self-help or by education: some decision or action by the other country in a relatively short time span is required. Of course, we cannot always get everything we want. But we will be more successful in formulating policy—we will

---

* Because influencing a government involves influencing a number of people, not an "it," I refer to a government as "they" or "them" even though with the word "government" I use a singular verb. This adaptation of a British practice, if somewhat inconsistent and occasionally jarring, may serve to remind the reader that people are involved and that, as Robert Southey wrote in 1817, the "Government are acting like themselves" (Life and Correspondence, vol. IV, p. 239).

get more and get it more efficiently—if we perceive our task as getting *them* to make a choice which is as good a decision as we can expect from them, all things considered.

THE DECISION WE WANT IS TO BE FORMULATED, NOT FOUND

The fact that in any conflict our objective can be perceived as a decision which we want another country to make does not mean that such an objective exists in the abstract. It does not have a pre-perception existence. People ask, "What is our objective in Vietnam?" as if by the scientific scanning of our minds we could discover "the American objective." In the long run we have, of course, certain values as objectives: peace, prosperity, self-determination, human welfare, self-fulfillment. But to work toward the realization of these values—to get anything practical accomplished— the objectives which we should pursue are things to be wisely formulated, not things to be found.

The formulation of decisions which we would like other countries to make should be a conscious task in the conduct of our foreign affairs, something to be pursued with art and skill. We should develop alternative formulations of an objective and then, taking into account the probabilities of success and the comparative costs and benefits, select a strategy which seems best to serve our conflicting and ambivalent interests. Our objectives (desired decisions) should be frequently re-examined to determine whether an alternative formulation might not serve us better. When we know what it is that we want them to say or do, then we can begin to take effective steps to get them to do it. We should formulate decisions which we would like others to make over various time spans. It is useful to know what we want that we can reasonably expect to get this week, this month, and this year. We can better explore the problem of how to get what we want in the Middle East or Africa by asking not, "What are our objectives?" but rather, "How ought we to formulate our objectives?"

Since it is their decision which we want to influence, and since they are the ones who will have a choice, it is their state of mind which is crucial. The focus of our policy is their decision. Our job is to so alter their perception of their choice that they will decide in the way we prefer. How they feel about the choice we will be asking them to make is just as important to us as how we feel about it. Typically the taking of international action concentrates first on domestic political feelings and limitations. What is it that we want? The views which are prevalent in the press, around the country, and in the various departments of government are reconciled, and a statement is produced. Such a statement is often issued without conscious attention to who it is that we want to make a decision, to what the decision is that we want and can expect them to make, or how we propose to go about convincing them that they ought to make it. The starting point should, instead, be the political problems of those we are trying to influence. What is their view of the situation? Can we say anything which will affect that view—affect their political problem? If we are trying to influence the Arab states, what domestic political problems do they have? What kind of a decision can we formulate which will be practical for them in their terms?

A government often acts with mixed motives. Physical self-help designed to prevent the Vietcong from seizing control of South Vietnam was also designed to influence the North Vietnamese to decide that the benefits of continued support to insurgents in the South were not as great as the costs. Bombing bridges in North Vietnam was intended both physically to prevent infiltration by making transportation difficult and to influence the government of North Vietnam to make a decision to reduce or stop infiltration.

When we are using such physical measures, it is easy to become confused about what we hope to accomplish and how. If we are to exert influence on another government, there must be at least some decision which they can make which will be favorable to us. If we ourselves do not know what it is we want them to do, or promise to do, we cannot expect to persuade them to do it. The ambiguity of our real objectives is illustrated by a hypothetical case. Suppose Fidel Castro called up the President and said, "Mr. President, economic sanctions have gone on long enough. You win: send down your terms. I will sign anything you can realistically expect me to sign. You must be practical—I have domestic problems. I am not going to commit political suicide. But anything within the realm of reason, I will sign." How long would it take the United States to prepare such a draft? How many weeks would it require to figure out what the United States would like to have happen in Cuba which it could reasonably expect to have happen and which its influence might bring about? The United States undoubtedly has a list of objectives with respect to Cuba, involving compensation for property taken, renunciation of Communism, removal of all Soviet and Chinese military and political personnel, and abandonment of all attempts to support revolution and wars of liberation in Latin America. This is not a decision we can realistically expect the Cuban government to make. We have devoted too little thought to what within the realm of the possible we would like to have happen in Cuba in response to our sanctions. Economic and political ostracism of the country may be justified in terms of its impact elsewhere in Latin America, but surely there are some modifications in the behavior of the Cuban government which it would be both reasonable and in our interests to try for. The failure to identify, at least to ourselves, some realistic objectives makes it less likely that we will be able to achieve any objective at all. If we insist on all or nothing, and have not got the capacity to get all, we get nothing. If there is no decision within the realm of the possible which both we and the government of Cuba know would result in the end of sanctions, then sanctions are like the weather and are unlikely to produce a political decision.

Another case is South Africa. Many well-intentioned people and governments are trying to organize economic sanctions against South Africa. There have been efforts to boycott American banks which have investments in South Africa. One may agree that the South African racial policy of apartheid is brutal and unfair and still ask the purpose of the sanctions. What is the theory of how a reduction in the economic prosperity of South Africa will help the lot of the blacks? Apparently, economic prosperity is one factor tending to cause blacks to be promoted despite the apartheid policy. There is almost no thinking about how economic "pressure" is supposed to cause South Africa to change its racial policies. No one has identified a decision which they would like the South African government to make, which they might realistically be persuaded to make, and which would be worth the effort.

Since in any international conflict our object is to exert influence on another country to make a decision we would like them to make, our actions, like those of a matador, have meaning only when we know what it is we would like our adversary to do. We must take into account our own long-range values, their view of the present conflict, their political problems, and their desires and fears, and to formulate some things we would like them to decide if we could convince them to do so. What kinds of things do we want? What would it be possible for them to decide? Can we make such a decision look attractive to them, or the consequences of not making the decision look costly? These are questions we should ask ourselves rather than "What is our foreign policy?"

2

Give Them a Yesable Proposition

ANY lobbyist knows that his chances of successfully influencing a government are increased if he has a specific proposal in mind. No one would expect success if he approached his own government and asked them to work out some scheme which reflected various principles. Less widely recognized is the extent to which obtaining an effective decision depends on presenting a proposal in the most readily decidable form. We are more likely both to know what we want and to get it if we try to write out the proposed decision with such clarity that it is in a form to which the single word "yes" would be an effective answer.

Putting our objective in the form of a yesable proposition makes us think through our position and the ways in which we will want to go about exerting influence. Too often our demand—the decision we desire—is vague simply because our own thinking is vague. Events have not forced us to be specific, and we have failed to recognize the impact which a specific offer or requested decision might have. We will almost always have a better chance of getting something we want if we know some specific things we would like to have.

There are costs in trying to develop a yesable proposition. Within the bureaucracy there is resistance to being specific. For the individuals concerned it involves work and risks with no compensating advantages. To reconcile the opinions of various officials and departments within our own government will take time and effort. But the more work we do, the easier time our adversaries will have making a decision we want them to make. Trying to write out some sample decisions which we would like Cuba or China or Algeria or East Germany to make in the next six months or next two years is a highly educational exercise. It should make us think about our conduct toward those countries. It tends to make us be realistic, to understand what is in the realm of the possible, and to bring the limitations of their political reality into the calculations of what we would like to have them do. It should help us reconcile what we want with what we can get. And it should make us think about actions we can take which will make it more likely that they will make some of those decisions. Whether or not we intend to communicate the specifics of our demand to our adversary, there is no excuse for not working out in our minds what it is we would like to have them say or do. To develop a firm governmental position might tend to freeze our position and cause us to be unduly rigid, but surely it is a useful exercise for each officer to write out one or two yesable propositions which he thinks are both desirable and within the realm of the possible. Unless we know what it is we are driving at, it will be pure luck if we are able to get it.

Communicating to another government exactly what it is

we would like them to decide also involves costs and risks. We may sound as if we were delivering an ultimatum and fail on that account. To submit one yesable proposition may be effectively to forfeit the opportunity to ask for more favorable terms. By being specific we risk including details which, though unimportant to us, make the entire proposition unacceptable to the other government. Coming forward with draft language too soon may upset another government which would like to feel that they had more participation in the formulation of the decision.

Yet there are strong advantages in communicating a simple and decidable question to the government we are trying to influence. Essentially, these advantages flow from the fact that the more work we do the less work there is for them to do, and the more likely they are to do it.

Even in the simple case of selling, where the only question is "How much?" setting a price makes it easier for the buyer. Buying in an oriental bazaar is likely to be a slow process, particularly if each party waits for the other to make the first move. A supermarket simplifies the buyer's job by putting a price tag on every item in the store. This is work and requires a lot of decisions. It also means abandoning the chance to get a higher price even from someone who would be willing to pay more. The advantage lies in giving each buyer a take-it-or-leave-it choice. Even where it is understood that price is subject to negotiation, the person who sets the first price has the harder task. He must think not only about the price he is prepared to accept but also about the problem of adding or subtracting an amount for the purpose of negotiating strategy. He must formulate a price from an almost unlimited number of possibilities, some of which are indistinguishable for all practical purposes. The second person has a far simpler choice.

For more complicated situations the difference between giving somebody a problem and giving him a yes-or-no choice is even greater. We can beat with a stick a donkey who is out in the pasture and perhaps convince him that there are carrots in the barn, but unless he sees a door into the barn, our efforts will be in vain. Any lobbyist knows that those he is seeking to influence must have a clear idea of what they are being asked to decide. It is not enough to present a government with alternative consequences: "If you do nothing about your population problem, you will be ruined; if you solve it, you can have economic growth and prosperity." The government will clearly prefer the' second set of consequences to the first, but no decision will result. There is nothing to which they can say "yes" which will get them there. A memorandum to a government official which makes a particular proposal and ends

Yes ____
No   ____

is far more likely to produce a decision than one which points out a problem and suggests that something ought to be done about it.

What is likely in the case of a decision by an individual is even more likely in the case of a decision by a group of individuals such as those who constitute a government. Here the difficulties of group decision are superimposed upon the difficulties which each member of the group would face in reaching a decision by himself. Within a bureaucracy, those who have worked out a specific plan and come forward with a yesable proposition are likely to carry the day.

The deliberations leading up to the Bay of Pigs disaster provide a good example of the importance of developing yesable propositions. President Kennedy's decision to go ahead with that operation against Cuba was no doubt affected by the fact that on one side he was presented with a well-staffed proposal in a yesable form. If the President accepted the recommendation of the Central Intelligence Agency, things would happen. He would not immediately be presented with a host of additional problems to work out. On the other side the President was faced with a recommendation that instead of going ahead with the plan he "do something else." Apparently there were no specific suggestions as to what should be done with the Cuban refugees training in Guatemala, how the government should deal with the disclosure problem, and what public position the President should take to minimize the domestic and international political costs. If there had been equally well-prepared plans in equally yesable form for this alternative, the President's decision might well have been different.

Foreign governments are no different from our own in finding it difficult to digest abstract wisdom or policy guidance. They, too, have a tendency to decide on those courses of action which are the most decidable—the most digestible —in form. And when communicating to a foreign government it is particularly useful that the communication be clear-cut. Much international communication is like smoke signals in a high wind. The more ambiguous the message the greater the chance for distortion and misunderstanding. The more strained the relationship the more likely that an adversary will interpret an ambiguous proposal or demand in the worst possible light. By presenting another government with a specific draft—a yesable proposition—we can cut through some of the suspicion about our intentions and encourage them to evaluate the real costs and benefits of making the decision we want them to make.

Attempts from 1965 through 1967 to influence the white

government of Rhodesia provide examples of both kinds. Prime Minister Wilson sought to avoid the unilateral declaration of independence in November of 1965 by proposing a joint announcement of the appointment of a royal commission. After some discussions and negotiation, Ian Smith of Rhodesia was presented with a draft in a form to which his acceptance would have produced an operative decision. Although it proved unpalatable, it was highly digestible in form and apparently came close to forestalling the declaration of independence.

This was followed by a long period of sanctions during which there was rarely any decidable question open to the Rhodesian government. Once the Security Council had voted mandatory sanctions, Rhodesians must have been convinced that there was in fact no feasible decision they could make which would make any difference. They were being asked to work something out, if they could, to resolve the situation. No one was surprised that they failed to do so.

For years, the United States sought to influence the Hanoi government and the Vietcong leadership to abandon the war in Vietnam and to shift the conflict from the battlefield to the bargaining table yet gave them no mechanically easy way to do so. Although we wanted the firing to stop, we presented our adversaries with no yesable proposition which would have resulted in a cease-fire. We left to them the almost unmanageably difficult task of formulating a cease-fire which might have been acceptable to both sides. We made it clear that the cost of continuing to fight the war would be high. We held out some hope that peace might be reasonably attractive to them—we tried to convince them that there were "carrots in the barn." But we provided no door to the barn. We confronted them with no choice where the simple word "yes" would have ended the fighting on a basis which we might have expected them to accept. Had they wanted a cease-fire, there was none they could have accepted. The frequent request of the United States that North Vietnam indicate what it was prepared to do in order to stop the bombing of North Vietnam amounted to a suggestion that it was up to them to give us a yesable proposition.

We often excuse our failure to present a yesable proposition with the thought that if the other side really wanted to do what we want them to, they could let us know and something could be worked out. But we are not concerned with assessing the relative moral blame between governments; we are not concerned with which government is more at fault. We are concerned with what we can do to maximize the chance of our success. It may be that at any given time North Vietnam was unlikely to make the kind of decision we wanted. However small the chances were, they were further decreased by the way in which the choice was put to them.

Perhaps the clearest statement of the United States position was in the President's speech of September 29, 1967, the so-called San Antonio formula:

The United States is willing to stop all aerial and naval bombardment of North Vietnam when this will lead promptly to productive discussion. We, of course, assume that while discussions proceed, North Vietnam would not take advantage of the bombing cessation or limitation.

This was not a casually drafted statement. Walt Rostow, Special Assistant to the President, later explained that every word had a purpose and a meaning: discussions must be held "promptly," they must be "productive," and so forth. The President's statement was, however, a carefully

drafted answer to the wrong question. It was an answer to the question, "What should our policy be?" If we really wanted productive discussions to be held promptly, we should have said something which would have made that event more likely. As it was, it was not enough for North Vietnam to say that talks would be held promptly after attacks on North Vietnam stopped. The United States then engaged in extensive "probes" in an effort to determine what North Vietnam "intended" when it agreed that talks would be promptly held. Diplomacy was used not to influence North Vietnam into doing what we wanted but to search for some nonexistent governmental "intentions." United States conduct appeared to be based on the premise that the government of North Vietnam (contrary to all experience with governments) would not be affected by the choices open to it but had some immutable intentions—intentions that were unresponsive, that is, to anything except military measures.

Rather than identify a posture for us to adopt we should have identified the operational decision which we wanted and could expect from North Vietnam and then given them a yesable proposition. Rather than having confronted North Vietnam with a statement of our "policy," we could have made sure that they were confronted with a choice that both was mechanically simple and stood a good chance of being politically acceptable.

An illustration of the kind of yesable proposition which might have shortened the war in Vietnam would have been an invitation from some legitimate source to a specific conference to be held at a given time and place. For example, India, as Chairman of the International Control Commission, might have sent a note along the following lines:

> The following parties are hereby invited to send representatives to attend a meeting of the International Control Commission in New Delhi at the Ministry of External Affairs Building to be held for three weeks beginning at 10 A.M. local time on Monday, the 4th of next month.
>
> > The government of the Democratic Republic of Vietnam, Hanoi
> > The government of the Republic of Vietnam, Saigon
> > The National Liberation Front of Vietnam
> > The United States
>
> The governments of Poland and of Canada, being the other members of the Control Commission, have each already indicated their willingness to have a representative attend the meeting. The purpose of the meeting is to advise the Commission as to measures which might be undertaken (1) to establish and maintain a cease-fire throughout Vietnam, and (2) to implement the Geneva Accords of 1954.
>
> To facilitate the work of the Commission and to improve the prospects for peace in Vietnam, all parties are hereby requested to implement effective at 2:00 A.M. local time on Sunday, the 3rd of next month, a general reduce-fire throughout all Vietnam, such reduce-fire to include a cessation of all major offensive military action, including a ces-

sation of the bombing and other armed attacks against North Vietnam, it being understood that no party should take military advantage of the reduced military activities on the part of an adversary.

Any party not wishing to send a formal representative to the meeting may send an unofficial observer or may designate any person, including the representative of some other party, to convey their views officially or unofficially to the Commission, to others attending the meeting, or to both. The meeting will take place as scheduled whether or not all invited parties decide to attend the opening sessions, provided only that the Commission finds that the general reduce-fire is in effect in Vietnam.

A representative of the government of India will chair the meeting. There will be an opportunity for informal discussions as well as for formal statements of position and advice at scheduled sessions. Attendance at the meeting will be without prejudice to the legal or other position of any party. It is requested that no party make any public statement which might prejudge the work of the meeting and that any questions be raised with the chairman on the first day of the meeting.

Such an invitation would have asked each of the parties concerned to do two things: implement a general reduce-fire at 2:00 A.M. on the morning of the third and designate a representative to attend the meeting in New Delhi at 10:00 A.M. on the fourth. Each of the decisions would involve some complicating factors, but each is essentially the kind of a decision which a government can make on a yes-or-no basis. No doubt a better draft could have been prepared. Some complexity is required in order to make the decision of the invitees easy. This draft was designed to meet the requirement of the United States that a cessation of the bombing of North Vietnam be accompanied by some reciprocal reduction of fighting on the other side, and the requirement of North Vietnam that it not negotiate while the bombing continued. There is little doubt that with some encouragement the government of India would have been willing to issue such an invitation at almost any time in 1967.

The contrast between the President's statement of September 29, 1967, and the suggested note illustrates the difference between focusing our thinking around our decision and focusing it around the decision of those we are trying to influence. The President's statement was concerned with the simplicity of our decision; the draft note is concerned with the simplicity of their decision. The President's statement was designed to articulate a "policy" which could be defended at home and abroad and which could continue in effect for an indefinite period. The draft note was designed to produce an operational decision. The President's statement could be ignored; a note such as the draft could not be. Or North Vietnam could say that they agreed with the President's statement that productive discussions should be held promptly following the cessation of the bombing, and still nothing would happen.

The above example is not intended to prove that North Vietnam would in fact have accepted such an invitation or to prove that discussions if held would have been productive. It is intended to illustrate what is meant by a yesable proposition. It is intended to illustrate what I mean when I say it is their decision we should think about.

3

Making Threats Is Not Enough

INTERNATIONAL conflicts exist because one government is unhappy with what another government is doing or is planning to do. We can therefore at any particular time think of a conflict as an attempt by one government to influence another to do something or not to do something. In international conflict as elsewhere our first reaction to somebody's doing something we don't like is to think of doing something unpleasant to them. In South Africa, we do not like apartheid; we promptly think of stopping future investment in South Africa. We oppose the unilateral declaration of independence by the white minority in Rhodesia, so we plan economic sanctions against Rhodesia. We want North Vietnam to stop the military and political support they are giving to the Vietcong, so we bomb them. Egypt, being opposed to Israel and her policies, decides to block Israeli traffic through the Suez Canal and the Gulf of Aqaba. Our instant reaction is to make it un-

pleasant for those who are doing or threatening to do what we do not like. We cut off trade, stop aid, stir up public opinion, pass resolutions of censure in the United Nations General Assembly, and institute retaliatory bombing. Whether we think it through or not, the implicit goal of our action is to cause the other government to make some decision. We want to cause them to change their mind. Our action is effective or not depending upon how it affects people's minds.

Raising the cost to an adversary of pursuing the course of action we do not like may not, however, be a good way to exert influence. Imposing pain may not be a good way to produce a desired decision. This is particularly true when the international adversary is a government, which necessarily means a group, a committee, a bureaucracy. Obviously cost is not wholly irrelevant. It is most relevant where we are trying to prevent a decision which has not yet been made. Much of our strategy relates to such potential conflict. We make a highly credible threat in order to deter a government from doing something they had not yet decided

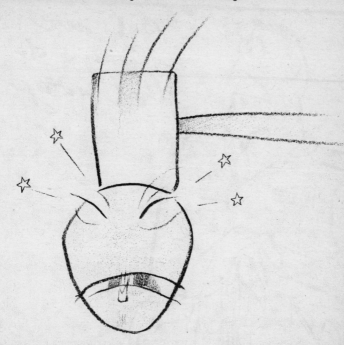

to do and perhaps had no-intention of doing anyway. The deterrent frequently appears to work. But a present conflict, as contrasted with a potential one, involves an attempt to change a government's mind. We want them to stop doing something they are doing, or to do something they are not doing. As a means of bringing about a change of intention, a foreign policy which concentrates on raising costs to an adversary is likely to prove both ineffective as to them and costly for us.

THE INEFFECTIVENESS OF INFLICTED PAIN

Inflicting pain upon an adversary government is, for a number of reasons, likely to be a poor way of getting them to change their mind. The government whose mind we want

to change anticipated some costs when they decided to do what we do not like. The costs which they anticipated were not sufficient to deter them. For us to inflict pain may simply be to impose costs which they have already taken into account. To act as they expected is hardly likely to cause them to reverse their position.

The theory of inflicting pain upon another country rests upon the premise that its government will change their mind in order to avoid further pain. Bombing power plants and other targets in North Vietnam, insofar as it was initiated for the purpose of producing a political decision, was carried out in order to make credible the threat of additional bombing. Present sanctions exert influence only if they communicate something about the future. They are intended to convey a convincing message that unless the decision we desire is made the situation will get worse. As in a labor strike, each day's infliction of pain is primarily for the purpose of communicating a vivid threat to inflict additional pain in the future. If the costs being imposed are no worse than those that had been feared, a government is given no reason to reverse their position.

To be sure, pain and costs in actuality may be more impressive than they were in contemplation. The government we are seeking to influence may have underestimated the actual consequences of economic sanctions or of a bombing program. It is equally probable, however, and perhaps more so, that imposed costs will seem less onerous in actuality than in contemplation. People adapt quickly to adverse circumstances. A future that might have looked intolerable is proved to be tolerable. The bombing of North Vietnam by the United States probably did more to convince the leaders of Hanoi that their economy could take it than it did to make the costs seem impossible to bear. The threat of B-52 bombings was perhaps more awe-inspiring than the bombings themselves.

Other considerations also suggest that inflicting pain upon an adversary may be worse than useless. There is a common tendency to treat sunken costs as invested capital. The greater the costs we impose upon our adversary, the greater the amount which they will regard themselves as having committed to their present course of action: "Having invested this much in the war of liberation, we cannot quit now. Having lost so many lives and most of our power plants, we should not now abandon the effort."

Finally, imposing additional costs may be like implementing a threat to kill hostages or prisoners of war: each cost imposed reduces the amount that could be saved by yielding to the demand. Suppose an adversary has twenty power plants. We bomb ten and say, "Will you quit now to save ten?" They refuse. We knock out five more and say, "Will you quit now to save five?" Although the marginal value of the remaining plants will have risen, our adversaries are likely to conclude that if they would not quit before to save twenty plants they should not quit now to save five.

To overcome these difficulties we are tempted to increase the amount of pain we impose. "So," we think, "they thought they could get away cheaply; we will show them how high the costs are really going to be." Can we, by thus imposing unexpectedly high costs, expect to change their minds?

The first problem is whether the higher costs are in fact unexpected. Our adversaries may have foreseen better than we what we would do. They are likely to think the worst of us. We are likely to be optimistic and to hope that modest efforts will be sufficient. This appears to have been the situation during the early stages of the bombing of North Vietnam. At a time when the bombing was still light and far removed from Hanoi and Haiphong, the government of North Vietnam spent a great deal of effort on building bomb shelters in Hanoi and on dispersing industry and population. The United States had made no decision to bomb Hanoi and presumably did not expect to do so. While we were presenting them with the vague threat of pain tomorrow if they did not change their mind today, they had in fact already decided not to change their mind even though the level of destruction increased substantially. As the United States stepped up its bombing program, it simply reached levels which had already been anticipated. Although our bombing program changed, the change had been expected. And we knew it had been expected. We should not have been surprised that it was an ineffective way of producing a change in North Vietnam's conduct.

Even where a change has been unexpected, a marginal increase in the costs we are inflicting is not likely to appear to them sufficient to justify reversing their decision. At any one time incurred costs are water over the dam. It is the increase in the threat that matters, and there, too, marginal changes are likely to be insignificant. Everyday experience illustrates the psychological difficulty involved in trying to change a person's mind by increasing the expected cost to him of continuing his actions. If my son is doing something even though I have threatened to spank him ten times for doing it, a threat to spank him twelve times is unlikely to produce better results. If I have decided to build a house at a rather high cost, my contractor knows I will not abandon the enterprise despite marginal increases in that cost.

With a group or a government, the problems are multiplied. First, there is a natural inertia which tends to prevent the reconsideration of decisions already taken—a past decision will continue to govern future conduct even though some of the facts change. Governments cannot reconsider a decision every day. And marginal changes in the cost rarely appear to justify putting a matter back on the agenda at all, since the new problem seems so much like the one already considered and disposed of. We may think that by increasing the pain a little bit every day we have made the adversary reconsider their actions every day. But they may never have seen a new decision as coming up for consideration at all. Their old decision simply continued to govern.

Even if increasing pain puts the matter back on their agenda, making the decision we want will look to them not like a new question but rather like the reversal of a decision already taken. We will be asking them to change their mind and back down because of a little more pain. It is even more difficult for a committee to abandon a course of action to which it has become committed than for an individual to do so, particularly in the face of what is sure to appear as blackmail. No individual in the group wants to be the coward who suggests that the best course might be to yield to pain and give up. Nobody wants to be the one who says, "It didn't work so let's change our policy. We made a mistake. Let's try something else." His status and his reputation among his colleagues are likely to be more important to him than any marginal contribution he might make to the national interest by sticking his neck out. Particularly in response to foreign pressure, any one member of the group may find it personally costly to suggest that the government ought to yield or otherwise to reverse their course. Each may keep his views to himself until it appears that the current of opinion for a change is running strong within the group. Under these circumstances actual support for a change may never be disclosed. If a committee is building a hospital, and the structure has progressed to the third floor when the builder comes in to inform them that the fourth floor will cost $100,000 more than anticipated, the committee is unlikely to abandon the project. The more gradual the escalation of cost the less likely that its increase will cause a change of position.

Discounting renders marginal increases in cost ineffective because an adversary will not be influenced by our doing what they more or less expected us to do. The threat of a drastic increase in pain is likely to be ineffective because it will not be believed. Another government will not be influenced by what they do not expect to happen. The threat of a small increase in bombing is always credible. But verbal threats of drastic escalation are looked at with doubt. Actions speak louder than words, and what we are doing now by way of imposing gradual rising costs suggests what we are likely to do in the future more clearly than can anything we say.

There is another and somewhat peculiar factor which makes it difficult for a government to reverse a decision taken in the face of a risk. A group which has decided to launch a project despite the *chance* that there will be high costs tends to confuse that decision with a decision to complete the project despite the *certainty* that the costs turn out to be high. A decision to start doing something which takes into account certain risks will be confused with a decision to proceed even though the risks materialize. It is impossible to articulate clearly those limited risks which a group of people are taking into account and the risks which they are not.

Examples will illustrate the phenomenon. Suppose a corporation is considering whether to start work excavating for the foundations of a building despite the fact that bids on the building have not yet come in. It is pointed out that

the excavation will cost only $50,000 and that if the build-
ing is to be built at all it will be highly desirable to save
time. The group discusses the risk that the bids will come
in high—so high that the entire plan should be reconsid-
ered. But the group decides to go ahead and start the excavating and to take that chance. Although the operative
decision was to risk $50,000 on the high probability that the
bids would be acceptable, such a group will almost certainly
later believe that they decided to "go ahead with the building" despite high costs—to build even if the lowest bid was
much higher than expected. A group decision on Friday to
buy groceries for a Sunday picnic despite the possibility of
rain will almost inevitably be understood on Sunday morning as a decision to go ahead on the picnic even though the
sky now looks threatening indeed.

This process undoubtedly worked on the group in Rhodesia which decided to declare independence despite the
small risk that sanctions would impose high costs. Increasing the bite of sanctions did not change their minds even
though the costs may have turned out to be much greater
than they thought probable. There were no doubt North
Vietnamese leaders who were aware of the risk of American
bombing when they first decided to step up infiltration.
They may later have thought that in deciding to go ahead
despite that risk they had decided to persevere after that
risk became a demonstrated certainty.

One further reason that increasing a threat, marginally
or drastically, does not usually work as well as we hope is
that our adversaries see that in carrying out the threat we
are hurting ourselves, too. To inflict pain involves a cost to
us as well as a cost to them. Carrying out a threat is something we do not want to do except to exert influence. The
same thinking which leads us to believe that imposing costs

on our adversaries will cause them to change their mind leads them to believe that the costs we are imposing on ourselves are likely to make us change our mind. The bombing of North Vietnam from mid-1965 to mid-1967 cost the United States at least $4 billion in airplane equipment alone. Whatever the monetary value of destruction we inflicted on North Vietnam during that period, it was almost certainly less than that. We looked at the destruction we had caused and could not understand why the rising cost of the war did not influence them to change their mind. They undoubtedly looked at the costs to us and were led to believe that they were so high that we would change our mind. They may have been wrong. But their political logic was as good as ours. Had we considered the net impact of the bombing as it appeared to them—in their eyes it was probably costing us more than it was costing them—we might have better understood the failure of the bombing to exert the kind of influence it was intended to exert.

INCREASING THE PAIN IS COSTLY TO US

Not only is threat making likely to be ineffective in persuading an adversary government to change their mind, it is likely to be unduly costly to us. It may seem as if we pay only modest costs in making a threat. We may look like a bully. Our international reputation as a leader whom others would like to follow may be damaged, and this may undercut our ability to continue to exert influence in the situation. Such immediate costs of our making a threat usually seem small if the threat is merely a verbal one. However, most of the threats we are discussing are "action threats," threats of carrying out future action which are communicated by the actions we are now taking and the pain we are now inflicting. Economic sanctions communicate a credible threat of further sanctions, bombing a threat of further bombing, and the breaking of diplomatic relations the threat of international isolation.

These threats by action involve greater immediate costs to us. First, there are out-of-pocket costs. Economic sanctions cost us lost trade and lost opportunities for future trade. It is expensive to maintain a huge military arsenal at the ready, or to mobilize and transport troops in order to show that we can and will use military force. The program of bombing in North Vietnam cost our economy a great deal. These out-of-pocket costs also represent opportunity costs—there are other useful ways to spend the resources, both at home and abroad. Second, since it is generally regarded as immoral to inflict pain simply to prove that you are willing and able to inflict it, we damage both our reputation and self-esteem. This immorality is so compelling that we will always advance some other justification for an action threat: we refer to it as interdiction, or retaliation, or even self-defense. Deliberate pain whose only justification is to extort a decision too closely resembles torture. If we did not have the interdiction rationale for the bombing of North Vietnam—the contention that our bombing of the North was not only to exert influence but also physically to prevent military supplies from reaching the South—the bombing would have been intolerably immoral both at home and abroad. This necessary gap between our primary motive of threatening future costs and our alleged justification results in a third cost, an almost inevitable "credibility gap," resulting from multiple and inconsistent explanations of military or other measures.

There are other costs of threat making inherent in the

international system. There are styles in international conflict: countries follow the precedents of others in the ways in which they seek to exert influence. A retaliatory raid by Israel may have more impact as an example than as a deterrent. Threats by one become a justification for threats by others. Reciprocal escalation is the consequence of two countries trying to influence each other by threats of demonstrated credibility. This style is costly and destructive to international order. It does not easily lead to solutions.

Another cost of threat making is that it diverts our attention from exactly what it is that we would like to have an adversary do. Britain devoted almost all its attention in the first year after Rhodesian independence to making economic sanctions "effective." Effectiveness was being measured in terms of the extent to which trade was being impeded, not in terms of the extent to which Rhodesians were being influenced to make a decision which Britain wanted. Almost no attention was devoted to the process by which a reduction in Rhodesia's economic welfare was supposed to convert that country into a functioning biracial democracy.

A decision to threaten and the later decision to implement that threat if the adversary fails to respond as we wish are two quite different matters. What exerts influence on an adversary is the risk of unpleasant consequences. They do not need to be certain that we will carry out a threat, nor do we. The fact that it is wise to make a threat does not mean that if our attempt to exert influence fails it will also be wise to carry it out. This is one reason why a decision to threaten is seductively attractive. The postponed costs are not immediately evident. We hope that the threat will be effective, in which case we will get something for very little. If it is not effective, it appears that we will still have open the choice of what to do then. Since that choice need not be made until later, it is easy at the outset simply to make the threat.

The real costliness of threat making lies in the fact that the postponed bills are likely to be large. If the threat fails, both courses open to us will probably be costly. Failure to implement our threat may reduce our credibility. We can afford to bluff occasionally without ruining our capacity to exert influence. But we cannot bluff every time without making future threats worthless. On the other hand, there are heavy costs in implementing the threat. The out-of-pocket costs are likely to be much larger than the costs of making the threat in the first place. More serious are the costs of doing something we have no reason for doing except that we said we would. There are, of course, some kinds of threats which we would like to carry out anyway: implementing that kind of threat may give us some actual benefit. But most of the threats we make in attempting to

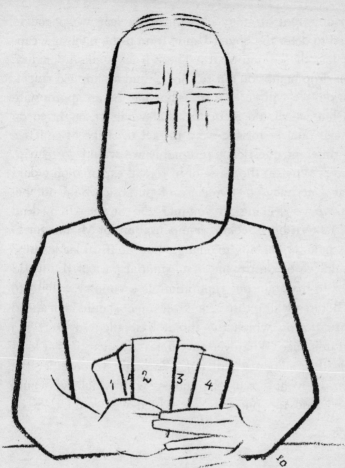

influence an adversary are threats of action we do not particularly want to take; such as stopping trade or aid, cutting off diplomatic relations, or taking military action. Once influence has failed it is to nobody's interest that we implement the threat except insofar as we need to in order to retain our credibility. Yet we are likely to take action harmful to both sides and may well accomplish nothing at all.

This problem is particularly acute in the case of our

nuclear-deterrent strategy. American nuclear weapons are intended to deter the Soviet Union from using nuclear weapons against the United States. There is an implied demand, "Do not drop bombs on our territory," and an implied threat, "If you do, we will go to war." This may be an appropriate threat, but we should recognize that what we ought to do if a Soviet nuclear missile were in fact to strike Miami is a totally different question. Presumably we would go to war. But why? "Why" in the sense of historical explanation would be clear, but "why" in the sense of purpose would not be. Would we be seeking to conquer the Soviet Union and occupy its territory? Seeking compensation for Miami? Seeking an apology? Seeking to change their political leadership? Or would we be destroying a substantial part of the world in order to maintain our reputation as a country willing to do so? Before making threats a government should look ahead to a situation in which the threat has failed to exert the desired influence. Whatever our offer and threat, it is at least possible that influence will fail. We ought to consider the position we would be in, the choices with which we would be faced, and the purposes for which we would then be acting.

A DECISION TO THREATEN BECOMES A DECISION TO IMPLEMENT THE THREAT

There is another reason why threats are costly and why we therefore ought to select with care the threats we make. The future option to bluff or to implement the threat is not as open a choice as it appears. A group tends to treat a decision to threaten as a decision to implement the threat even though analytically these are quite different decisions. We are likely to find ourselves dragged into the implementation of a threat we had no intention at all of implementing.

The bias in favor of implementing threats is another result of the inherent ambiguity of a decision which takes some future risks into account. The decision to make a threat presumably took into account the possibility that the threat would not work and that in such an event we *might* implement it. But a government will tend to treat that decision as a decision not to bluff—as a decision to carry out the threat if the occasion arises. There are a number of reasons for this. The first decision involves a risk within a risk—a risk that the threat will fail and that there will then be the risk of implementing it. This situation is sufficiently ambiguous so that the risks may merge. People will not realize that there is an opportunity for a new decision to be made in the light of new circumstances.

Further, a governmental threat (for example, "If Cuba seizes the oil refineries we will cut off all trade") sounds like a governmental decision. Subordinate officials will see themselves as having the power to implement such a policy but not to change it. There is no automatic occasion for a new decision. The bureaucracy is likely to proceed day by day toward carrying out the threat. The lack of an equally well-considered alternative to implementing the threat also operates to make any such possibility unlikely.

Confusion between the decision to make a threat and the decision to implement it is particularly costly where the threat is to do something for an indefinite period in response to some one-shot action. An example illustrates how one thing is likely to follow another without re-examination. Suppose a foreign government proposes to nationalize some American-owned property. In an effort to deter them we threaten to cut off all trade if they seize the property. To make the threat credible we suspend trade immediately. If the property is nationalized the initial decision to make the threat will be taken by most people in the government as a decision to cut off, and to keep cut off, all trade. Any official can continue the trade embargo for another day. That appears to be our "policy." A decision *not* to carry out the threat that failed will be regarded as a reversal of a prior decision. It will be difficult for someone to say: "They nationalized the property. That's water over the dam. Our threat failed, and we should now resume trade. We should now try for a different objective, such as compensation or some arrangements to protect other property not yet nationalized, and make threats or offers appropriate to our new purpose." Any termination of the embargo will be left to higher authority within the government. Higher authority will also tend to regard an end of the embargo as a reversal of policy. These open-ended punishments, which include things like nonrecognition and the breaking of diplomatic relations, are likely to continue indefinitely with no real purpose in mind and with no advance consideration of the circumstances in which we would expect to stop imposing them.

Often this kind of policy is justified in terms of teaching our adversaries a lesson. Hurting a country which has failed to do what we want is regarded as rational for educational reasons. Our adversaries and third parties are expected to learn something about us which is worth the investment and the risks: they will have learned that we are not likely to tolerate certain conduct, that if we make a threat we are likely to carry it out, and that there are some things they "can't get away with." History suggests that the value of such lessons tends to be exaggerated.

Perhaps no lesson will be learned at all. On another occasion our adversary is likely to believe that the circumstances

are different. There are so many variables in international affairs that one government is unlikely to give much weight to what another government did under different circumstances as an indication of what they are likely to do now. Reputations for toughness are ephemeral. What Khrushchev did in Budapest was not a reliable guide to what he would do in Cuba and even less reliable as an indication of what Kosygin might do in North Vietnam. Our adversary will place far greater weight on what we will be doing the next time— mobilizing men, moving men, moving planes, calling in congressional leaders—than on what we did before in a different setting.

Our adversary may in fact draw a conclusion directly contrary to the one we wanted. For us to implement a threat involves us both in a painful experience. Rather than learn their lesson, the adversary and third countries may assume that we have learned our lesson: it cost us so much we will not do it again. Looking at the difficulties in which the United States has found itself in Vietnam, would-be aggressors might conclude that the United States would be most reluctant to repeat such an experience and that they could now act with reduced fear of United States intervention.

An action which produces no more constructive result than punishment is likely to look like a failure. The apparent failure of punishing actions—military (as in Vietnam), economic (as with sanctions against Rhodesia), or political (as in the breaking of diplomatic relations with Britain by the African states)—may lead countries to believe that such punishing actions will not be repeated. Further, it is not clear that the failure to take a retaliatory action will teach our adversary that we are soft. They are perhaps as likely to think that having backed down once, we cannot afford to do it again. Retaliation may, it is true, placate the international community and relieve the pressure for vengeance exerted by our domestic population. But it may also aggravate the situation and make our adversary less accommodating. Many of our stubborn international differences result from actions that looked backward instead of forward. Such continuing policies as the nonrecognition of China and restrictions on trade with Cuba and with Eastern Europe involve substantial costs in terms of lost opportunities. Whatever the rationalization, each of these policies was adopted in response to the past action of another government rather than through a rational consideration of how we could best improve the situation in the future. Whenever such responses to the unwanted decision of another government are justified as necessary to maintain our reputation or to teach another nation a lesson, that justification should be examined with skepticism.

If we are trying by a threat to discourage another government from engaging in a one-shot bit of conduct, we should probably threaten a one-shot bit of retaliatory action. If the threat fails, at least we can implement it quickly and confront everyone with a *fait accompli*. The single air attack on North Vietnam in August, 1964, following the apparent attacks by North Vietnam on United States ships in the Gulf of Tonkin was retaliatory action of this one-shot kind in response to one-shot action by an adversary. (Unfortunately it also set a precedent for further raids.)

WE SHOULD MAKE THEIR CHOICE PALATABLE

So far I have suggested that governments frequently try to bring about a decision they want by increasing the cost to another government of not making that decision, and that this method of influence is both ineffective and costly. The palatability to an adversary of the choice we want them to make is affected not simply by the pain we threaten to inflict if they do not make the choice, but rather by the total combination of many elements. The set of consequences of doing what we want (including both the benefits and the disadvantages) must be more attractive to them in sum than the set of consequences which will ensue if they do not do what we want. The choice we present them must be palatable. This can be represented by the following map, in which the "offer" designates the entire set of circumstances, both good and bad, which the *adversary* believes will come about if

MAP

	DEMAND The decision desired by us	OFFER The consequences of making the decision	THREAT The consequences of not making the decision
WHO?	Who is to make the decision?	Who benefits if the decision is made?	Who gets hurt if the decision is not made?
WHAT?	Exactly what decision is desired?	If the decision is made, what benefits can be expected? —what costs?	If the decision is not made, —what risks? —what potential benefits?
WHEN?	By what time does the decision have to be made?	When, if ever, will the benefits of making the decision occur?	How soon will the consequences of not making the decision be felt?
WHY?	What makes this a right, proper, and lawful decision?	What makes these consequences fair and legitimate?	What makes these consequences fair and legitimate?

Every feature of an influence problem can be located somewhere on this schematic map. The nature of a given problem can be discovered through estimating how the presumed adversary would answer the above questions.

they make the decision we are asking them to make, and the "threat" indicates the set of consequences, as they see them, of their not making the decision.

The set of questions we ought to be asking about each of these elements—the decision, the offer, and the threat—will enable us to analyze how the choice we are presenting looks to the country we are trying to influence and what we can do to alter the scheme so as to be more effective in getting them to make a decision. Who is it we are asking? On whom will the consequences fall if they do not make the desired decision? Will they fall on the same "who" as the group we are asking to make the decision? What is the decision we are asking them to make? What is it that we are saying will happen if they do or do not make it? When will these consequences occur? And why are we asking for this decision— is it a legitimate request, a reasonable demand? Are there reasons that they ought to make that choice? If they are "bad," why would implementing the threat be legitimate?

These are questions which the map presents. It does not provide any answers. It is a simple scheme which can be applied to any kind of conflict—marital problems, domestic disputes, or business dealings. It is not unique to international affairs. The proposition of this book is that by asking about the international conflicts in which we are engaged some of the simple questions indicated by the map—by rigorously asking the simplest questions—a significant improvement can be made upon the present style of foreign policy. The object of our policy is to cause someone else to make a decision. To do so we must alter the decision or the consequences of making it and of not making it so that they will now see the total choice in a favorable light. It is their perception of what is in the boxes on the map that is crucial, not ours. Our task is to change their perception by arranging the desired consequences so that, on the basis of the total attractiveness of the combination of all the boxes on the map, they will want to make that decision.

Changing the threat by increasing the threatened pain— military deterrence, damage infliction, weapons development, threats of sanctions—encompasses only half of one box in the threat column. These are the undesirable consequences to the adversary of not making the decision we want. (As they see it, there will of course be desirable consequences, too.) Herman Kahn's book *On Escalation* is essentially forty-two ways to change the way this box looks to an adversary. He suggests how to make the consequences of being "bad" look less attractive, more immediate, or more probable. That entire book is about escalating a threat for the purpose of exerting influence. We need equally detailed books dealing with the problems of whom we are trying to influence, what we want them to do, and how to make that look attractive. Successful influence depends on a consideration of all parts of this map, not just one, and on a consideration of how the various parts ought to be coordinated.

Even when considering only the threat, there may be more effective means of exerting influence than to change the level of threatened pain. One way to change the threat is to make it more immediate, to change the timing. We may not want the threat to appear as an ultimatum, because then its legitimacy would be reduced and the adversary might balk. But we may be able to advance the time at which the disadvantages of their not changing their minds will take effect. Or we might change the threat so that it will fall more directly on those who are being asked to decide. A lunch-counter sit-in is a more effective way to get a business to desegregate than a street march in part because the threat is calculated to fall directly and immediately on those who are being asked to make a decision. We may change the threat so that instead of imposing costs it appears to deprive the decision maker of benefits he had already anticipated. Again, the lunch-counter sit-in is a good example of this technique. Or we may change the nature of the threat for the purpose of getting the decision back on their agenda, so that we present them with what appears to be a choice with quite different dimensions. A more legitimate threat is likely to be more effective. For example, a threat by an international body may exert far more influence than the same threat from an adversary government. Any one of these methods of changing a threat may be more successful in getting an adversary to change their mind than increasing the magnitude of the pain we are promising to inflict on them.

An element which is unimportant to us may be important to an adversary. One of the sticking points of international conflict is that each party thinks that because they regard some issue as unimportant it will be easy for the other party to back down on it. But it is the adversary's perception of what is important which controls their decision, not our perception or some objective standard. No matter how irrational they may be, if we want to influence them, we should deal with them on their own ground; deal rationally with their irrationality. If they prefer prestige to economic welfare, an effective policy will offer them prestige. They may be more influenced by the name attached to a million-dollar aid program than by the fact that it is being offered. The irrationality of an adversary does not make the map irrelevant; it makes all the more important our consciously considering how the various elements may look to them. What do they think we are asking them to decide, what do they think the consequences will be, and how do they value those consequences?

Consider, for example, the choice faced by North Vietnam in May of 1966, as their leaders may have seen it. One of the decisions with which they were faced each day was whether to say that they were willing to negotiate. This was the "demand" of the United States. For this particular decision we can focus our attention on two important boxes: the consequences as they looked to Hanoi of making the decision we wanted and the consequences of not doing so. The table on page 53 suggests how these may have looked to them.

It is not surprising that given this view of the consequences of the decision we were asking them to make, they did not make it. The task of an effective policy maker would have been to examine this list and decide what *we* could do which would change one or more of the elements that were significant in *their* eyes in order to make it more likely that they would make a decision we wanted.

To arouse maximum support at home we usually insist that a dispute is a conflict of principle. But if we want success we should look for a solution consistent with the principles of our adversary as well as our own. By so arranging matters that an adversary government can go along without abandoning their principles, we make it easier for them to do so. My premise is that most international objectives can be achieved only by something more than our own actions: by having other governments make decisions. If this is so, both we and our adversaries must prefer the decision we want them to make to its alternatives. If only we prefer it, they will not make it; if only they prefer it and want to make it, then it would not be a goal of our policy. Unless there is some common ground there is no hope for influence. We seek to make it appear to them that the sum of the consequences of going along is profitable enough for them to make the decision—that is, it is better than the sum of the conse-

THE OFFER

(Consequences of saying
"We will now negotiate")

Benefits

Bombings. A chance that bombing will stop (but U.S. may insist on continuing until there is a "verified end of infiltration").

Casualties. A chance of negotiating a cease-fire (but Saigon and U.S. may insist on continued "pacification" in the South as talks go on).

Negotiations. A chance of real talks (but they may be frustrated by Saigon or by a dispute over representation of the Liberation Front).

Costs

Ruined morale. To talk about talks now would undercut our fighting morale while the fighting continues.

Giving in. To negotiate now is to give in to U.S. blackmail tactics.

No victory. To negotiate is to abandon the opportunity for an impressive victory over forces of imperialism.

No unification. To negotiate is almost certainly to abandon the unified Vietnam to which all agreed.

No socialist South Vietnam. U.S. cannot be expected to agree to a socialist South Vietnam (cf. Dominican Republic).

Foreign-dominated South. To negotiate means continued domination by neocolonialists against which so many have fought for so long.

Bad precedent. Successful U.S. blocking of a war of liberation will make imperialist intervention more likely elsewhere.

THE THREAT

(Consequences of *not* saying
"We will now negotiate")

Costs

Bombings. Will increase, with a serious risk to Hanoi and Haiphong.

Casualties. Our high losses may rise from X per week to Y per week unless we revert to more guerrilla-like tactics.

Negotiations are postponed for at least one more day.

Benefits

Possible quick victory. An excellent chance that Saigon government will completely fall apart or that U.S. will quickly pull out because of criticism at home and abroad. Either would assure us a quick and complete victory.

Certainty of eventual success. This is a contest of will. The Vietnamese people fighting for their own country, for freedom from foreign domination, and for the socialist society of the future will certainly outlast alien, neocolonialists who try to stop political forces with bombs. We will tolerate high casualty rates longer than they, and thus win.

Loyalty to principle. To fight on is to adhere to our values and principles.

World-wide respect for standing up to the American goliath.

Option to negotiate later. If at any time it seems wise to negotiate, we can do so on terms no less favorable than now.

quences of not going along. In game-theory terms this is simply saying that international conflicts are not zero-sum games.

WHO?

The first question on the map is "Who?" Who is it we would like to have make a decision? After Rhodesian independence the British government did not articulate clearly the target of their sanctions, nor was there public discussion of the effect of their policy on the people they claimed to be influencing. Sanctions were intended to make it hard on "Rhodesia." Recognizing that Rhodesia was simply a piece of geography, the British government said that it was the politically responsible community leaders within Rhodesia who were the precise target of influence. The sanctions were

presumably aimed at a typical business man in Salisbury—
perhaps a banker with political experience.

Put such a man in the upper left-hand box and suppose
that he is the "who" we are trying to influence. It is then
the consequences to him that are crucial. What is his choice?
He gets up in the morning, reads the newspaper, and says
to his wife, "I see that Harold Wilson wants us to return to
constitutional government, and I suppose he is talking to me.
Perhaps I had better go down to Government House and tell
them that I am prepared to return to constitutional government. But if I do, what will happen? I will go in and the
British Governor will ask, 'You and who else? Do you have
the support of the army? Did you bring others along?' And
I will have to say, 'No.' Then he will say, 'When there are
enough of you, let me know.' I will walk out and quite likely
be picked up and put under house arrest like others of whom
the government is suspicious." The consequences to such a
man of making the decision Britain was asking him to make
were considerably worse than the consequences of not making it. Britain was not offering him any benefits for making
the decision.

Making effective policy lies in the coordination of the boxes
—the demand, the offer, and the threat—to make an adversary's choice easy and desirable in his eyes. Once we know
whom we are trying to influence, we should see whether we
are making the offer and threat to the same person or group.
In Rhodesia, the first effects of economic sanctions fell on the
blacks, who had no voice in any government or private decision making and about whom those with responsibility for
changing the course of independence cared little. On the
other hand, in Ceylon the government was successfully influenced by the offer of the United States to resume economic
aid if the government worked out with a United States oil

company a satisfactory arrangement for compensation. Although the offer was directed at the people of the country (no aid, theoretically, would go into the pockets of government officials), the government was deeply interested in the aid. The critical point is the nature of the influence exerted by the offer and by the threat on that group to which we are presenting a choice.

WHAT?

The second question is "What?" What is it we want them to decide? What do they perceive will be the consequences of making that decision (the offer), and what do they perceive will be the consequences of not making it (the threat)? If it is their decision that counts, they must know of the decision we are trying to get them to make. The more mechanically easy it is to make that decision—the more yesable the proposition with which we confront them—the more likely they are to make it.

What is the offer? What do they see as the advantages (and disadvantages) of the situation which they would be in if they went along with us and made the desired decision? In Vietnam, for example, we offered fair elections, economic-aid programs, various levels of American disengagement and withdrawal. There are two questions to be asked about such benefits we are promising to extend to them if they make a desired decision. First, are these benefits things which are really attractive to them? If we are trying to influence a donkey with carrots, it will be important to know if the donkey likes carrots. Equally important is the problem of convincing the donkey that if he performs he will actually get some carrots. The credibility of an offer is just as important as the credibility of a threat—even more important, if the analysis of a later chapter is accepted. It costs a great deal to make threats credible. It may be that we can exert as much influence by doing things which are easier and less expensive and are designed to convince an adversary that we are in fact committed to our offers. Again, since it is their perception that is important, we should perhaps devote more effort than we now do toward convincing them that we will in fact do what we say we will if they go along with us.

Another way to improve an offer is make the disadvantages of going along appear less costly. This may involve what is called saving face, but the problem is broader than that. In making the decision we want, they will suffer domestic and international costs. We can exert influence by acting to minimize these costs.

WHEN?

The third question is "When?" The decision we are asking them to make will be more palatable if the threat and the offer are well correlated to the time at which the decision is required. When American bombing of North Vietnam began in 1965, there were spokesmen for our government who said, "We do not want their promises, nor do we expect North Vietnam to stop its support for the Vietcong immediately. The decision we want them to make is to taper off over the next three months." If that was true, the message was demonstrably wrong in its timing. It was, "Slow down your support over the next three months or we will bomb you tomorrow." My young son laughs at me when I say, "No television tonight unless you are good next week." He knows that I have to decide before he does.

WHY?

The last question is "Why?" The word is used here in the sense of seeking justification. Is our demand justifiable? How legitimate is it in our adversary's eyes? In terms of morality and humanity, international law, and past actions by ourselves and our adversaries, how justifiable does our demand appear to them?

Legitimacy is usually considered to be icing on the cake. But the legitimacy of our demand as perceived by an adversary is important. They will be more likely to make a decision if it appears legitimate to them. This is true not only because an adversary will see that we can win third-party support for a legitimate demand. Every government must also consider their internal situation. An adversary government must justify their decisions to their own people; they are constrained at least in part by what their own citizens will say about the decision. Also governments and government officials are influenced by what they themselves think is right. Most government officials want to do the right thing by their own standards. No matter how wrong we think our adversary is, we can best see how to influence them by realizing that they think they are on the side of right. Part of exerting influence is convincing them that to make the decision we want them to make would be the right thing to do in terms of the values accepted by them. This is another aspect of the proposition that solving a conflict involves an attempt to get them to make a decision which both is favorable to us and appeals to them.

Similarly, a threat can be legitimate if its implementation would be morally or legally justified. Such a threat is more likely to exert influence than one which appears to be rank blackmail.

WE ARE TRYING TO CHANGE THEIR MIND

Asking such questions should help identify the reasons why our attempts at influence have so often failed. We are not surprised that North Vietnam did not make a decision to indicate that it was willing to negotiate in May, 1966. Although the foregoing list is merely descriptive, it provides a base for considering what ought to have been done. It draws attention to consequences we might have tried to change. And if someone proposes a new way of exerting influence, the map provides a way of appraising the new method's chance of success.

In any conflict, we can look at the situation knowing that the balance of consequences has not yet been sufficient to cause the adversary to make the decision we would like him to make; otherwise he would already have made it. At any one time the question is, What aspects of their perceived choice can we change in order to make them change their mind? If it is proposed to induce North Vietnam to agree to negotiate by increasing their casualty rate, we can look at the list and try to guess how North Vietnam would react if they were faced with the prospect that fighting on would increase the rate of casualties not from X to Y but from Y to Z. Could we expect that change to make the decisive difference? What other elements ought to be changed, and how can we do it?

Using the map we can see that threat making is not everything. It is just one of a number of considerations we should be taking into account.

4

Ask for a Different Decision

WE NEVER start out with a clean slate. Any conflict grows out of a situation in which a government had a choice of doing what we wanted them to do but did not do it. In order to exert influence on them, we must change some aspect of the choice with which they see themselves as being faced. Rather than trying to change the threat—the consequences which will follow from their continuing not to make the decision we seek—we may be more successful if we change the decision we ask them to make. That is, we can redefine the demand rather than try to change the consequences they expect from failing to meet our demand. In the short run we will be unable to change their basic values or attitudes. In Chapter 3 I suggest that changing the threat—the consequences we promise them if they do not make the decision we are asking for—may be ineffective and worse than useless, for it may involve serious costs to ourselves. By presenting them with a different proposed decision, we can present them with a decision which we want and which they are more likely to make.

We do not know the exact reasons they did not make the decision yesterday. It may be that what we wanted was so odious to them or so inconsistent with their own objectives that they will never make that decision, no matter how much we can offer them to be "good" or how much we threaten them if they are "bad." In such a case, changing the demand to one which is more internally acceptable to them is the only way to get something we would like. Whether or not that is the case, there are persuasive reasons for changing the decision we are asking them to make.

First, we can put the matter back on their agenda. We have seen that a government tends to conform to a "policy decision" to pursue a certain course of action, even though the costs change. A government which has made a decision is unlikely to reconsider the wisdom of that decision every day. If North Vietnam has decided not to negotiate, a change in the casualty rate will probably not of itself cause any one North Vietnamese official to reopen that decision. On the other hand, if a fresh proposal comes in, a new decision is required. Consider the example of an organization which goes to a congressman with a proposed bill and a petition signed by a thousand voters asking him to support the bill. The congressman says no. The organization will not be likely to achieve success by simply coming back with 1,200 names. But if it comes back with a revised Paragraph 6, the congressman has a new decision to make. Likewise, if General DeGaulle were to have invited the North Vietnamese to send a representative to a conference in Paris to discuss the Vietnam situation, the government of North Vietnam would have had a slightly different decision to make than the one they had previously made "not to negotiate." The matter would have been up for reconsideration. The whole question of negotiating would have been raised anew because a different demand had been made. The chances of a favorable decision would have been greater than otherwise simply because a new choice—whether or not to send the representative—would have been required.

Second, changing the demand means that a favorable decision now does not require a reversal of a previous decision. The matter is not only back on the agenda, but in order to decide our way they need not admit that the prior decision was wrong. We saw that it is extremely difficult for a government to reverse themselves. Individuals who now believe the decision was wrong when made, or realize they have been proved wrong by events, often feel bound to respect the decision nevertheless. I was once present at a meeting of fifteen or twenty government officials considering how to implement a minor presidential decision. The best way anyone had thought of for doing so was not very satisfactory. When the presiding officer asked how many thought that the President ought to be told he had made a mistake and advised to reverse his decision, no one spoke up. Then, in an unusual move, the question was put differently. If the President *were* to reconsider his decision, how many of those present would advise him to go ahead with the decision? No one. The reluctance to urge the reopening of a decision once made was so great that even though no one in the room then believed the decision to have been a good one on the merits, it was almost carried forward without objection. Coming in from the outside with a different proposal tends to get around this bureaucratic reluctance to reverse prior decisions.

By holding rigidly to a particular demand, such as "54'40° or fight" or "release the *Pueblo* and its crew immediately," the public can more readily be convinced that the objective is important and that the government is committed to it. The longer we go forward with our demand unchanged, the more difficult it becomes to change it. There are some advantages to this. We may acquire the traditional bargaining strength of a man with a hardhearted partner ("I personally might go along with your case but our public opinion would never stand for it"). But rigidity promotes rigidity. And a little flexibility on our part makes possible greater flexibility on theirs. Therefore, a third reason for a government's changing their demand is to keep themselves unfettered by domestic opinion and free to pursue objectives which seem wise in the light of developing circumstances.

There is little value in continuing to ask for decisions which have already proved unattainable. In one sense American public opinion, dead set against recognizing Communist China, "strengthened" the government's hand. But it did so by tying it up. There is reason to believe that at times over the past fifteen years the government would have adopted a more flexible policy toward China but for domestic opinion. One way for a government to keep themselves from being boxed in by domestic opinion is to make modest changes and reformulations in their stated objectives. During the course of the fighting in Vietnam in 1965 the internal debate began to polarize around two positions which came to be identified as "winning" and "losing." The peace offensive of December, 1965, did not simply demonstrate to other governments that we were interested in Vietnam negotiations. The Administration's insistence that there was no single solution in Vietnam to which the United States was committed served to loosen up internal debate. It became easier for senators and others to question the objective of military victory and to suggest alternatives. The government acquired a greater scope of action. Manipulation of domestic opinion by governments is decried; leadership is not. One way to lead the public in a democracy is for a government to re-examine and reform their objectives often enough to avoid rigidifying the country's position and often enough to encourage free discussion of what those objectives ought to be.

There are disadvantages to changing the demand. By changing it we indicate a willingness to change it again. The adversary government may believe that if they hold firm we will ultimately make a demand which is even more

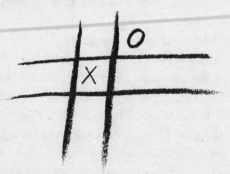

attractive to them. During 1945 the Allies demanded "unconditional surrender" from Japan. In hindsight it is apparent that we were asking for more than we needed and that on such questions as the Emperor's future we had made it unnecessarily difficult for the Japanese government to yield. If in early 1945 we had shifted and offered a package proposal which embodied the substance of the MacArthur Constitution, which was actually imposed on Japan, it would have been more attractive to them. In theory, it should have been easier for them to yield. But to move from a demand for unconditional surrender to one for acceptance of a more modest demand might have caused Japan to believe that the terms would continue to improve with time. So long as our demand remained rigid for unconditional surrender, there was little chance of their thinking we might make a better offer. In general, however, we are likely to be more successful in exerting influence by changing the decision we are asking our adversary to make than by changing the consequences to them of making it.

The way in which governments presently formulate policy demonstrates not only that domestic political considerations

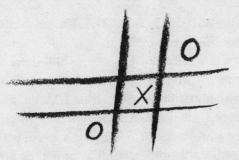

are often given undue importance but also some common errors which reflect the fact that few people have thought through what foreign policy is all about. One error, as suggested, is not to identify any demand at all; we often fail to suggest what it is that we want an adversary to say or do. Our adversary must then judge our purpose from the various things we have, at some time or another, publicly said or done. The more hostile the general relationship between us and our adversary, the worse the interpretation the adversary is likely to make of our words and deeds. Vietcong leadership probably believed that the United States was demanding what would be, in effect, unconditional extermination. The South African government probably believes that those imposing sanctions are demanding that the country be turned over immediately and completely

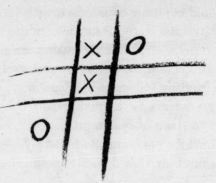

to black-nationalist mob rule. The United States may be operating on the assumption that nothing short of world domination will satisfy the Chinese, while those in the Chinese government probably assume that we are demanding they accept domination by the United States and abandon their communist ideology. And so on. The interests of different nations are inconsistent enough even with the best of understanding. Misunderstanding promotes needless conflict. The difference between our perceptions does provide, however, an opportunity for us to exert influence at no cost. By simply letting the other government know what we really want instead of what they think we want, we will make the decision we desire more likely. To understand how to alter the demand we are making, we should examine their present view of the decision they would have to make in order to produce one set of consequences (the offer) rather than another (the threat).

A second common error is to make an entirely unrealistic demand, to ask for some decision we cannot have the slightest expectation of getting them to make. Here factual knowledge about the other country is critical. What kind of decisions are they able to make? What questions are open and which questions are, for practical purposes, closed?

None of the African countries which support sanctions against South Africa know what they would like to have happen there that, in their wildest hopes, might actually happen. Their sanctions presumably represent a threat that "something bad will happen unless ____." Unless what? Abandon racial discrimination? That is an entirely unrealistic demand. In the nineteen-fifties and early sixties the American position on Eastern Europe suffered from the same error. We refused to trade because they were Communist. Our implicit demand was that they abandon Communism in order to be able to trade with us. No one thought that objective realistic, yet we pursued it. In many cases it is necessary to change our demand simply in order to ask for something which is within the realm of the possible.

A third common error is to make unnecessarily ambiguous demands. As we will see, demands which are purposely ambiguous or leave room for interpretation by an adversary are sometimes effective; we may want to be more or less

specific depending on the circumstances. But as the discussion of yesable propositions should have made clear, one requirement of the successful conduct of foreign affairs is routinely to work out, at least for ourselves, some *specific* things we would like to have an adversary do or promise to do.

ASK SOMEONE ELSE

As suggested, one of the first questions we ought to ask ourselves in trying to produce a decision is: Whose decision is it we are trying to affect? Within any government those making a decision must take some things as given and some as subject to their own choice. The more precisely we can focus attention on those we are trying to influence, the more accurately we will be able to make a judgment about what it is possible for them to do and what is beyond their capacity. Thus as a starting point it is useful to identify the existing object of influence.

One of the reasons we often make unreasonable demands is that we are, in effect, asking the wrong group within a country, the wrong country, or perhaps the wrong group of countries, and those we are asking to decide are unable or unwilling to make the decision we want. Our estimate of how much those we are presently asking take as given and not subject to change is approximate at best, since what it is possible for them to decide is partly a function of how hard they try. Having this in mind, we may want to let our reach exceed our grasp—but not by too much. Our chance of success will be enhanced if we can change our demand so that those we are asking to decide are capable of doing so. In the Cuban missile crisis it was usually quite clear when we were talking to Cuba and when to Moscow. We failed only when we asked Moscow to agree to on-the-ground inspection in Cuba, a demand on which the Russians could not, and therefore predictably did not, deliver. We had made a demand of a party which was not able to make the decision, and we wisely accepted the substitute of air surveillance.

The government of North Vietnam, for example, may have trained and supplied the Vietcong, organized, financed, and established the National Liberation Front, and directed the entire effort to overthrow the South Vietnamese government. But these military and political forces having been set in motion, it did not follow that the leadership in North Vietnam was able by itself to call off the entire war of liberation.

This example suggests that in selecting and in shifting the party on whom we try to exert influence, we should look ahead to the decision we want instead of looking back at those who may have caused the situation we do not like. The example also illustrates another common error. What is perceived in Saigon as one adversary may, for the purpose of making a decision, be better understood as two or more separate groups of decision makers subject to one another's influence. Outsiders almost invariably oversimplify the unity of the political body they are trying to influence. Israeli officials often refer to "the Arabs" as though they constituted a single political organization. In the aftermath of Israel's attack on the Beirut airport the Foreign Minister of Israel went further and spoke critically of the "attitude of the non-Jewish world to the Jewish world." Some people still talk of trying to influence "the Communist World" to abandon its aggressive ways or to reach some other decision, when it is abundantly clear that the numerous governments and revolutionary leaders who are thus lumped together rarely if ever reach a collective decision on anything. We are actually trying to exert influence on a host of independent and separate deciders. The lumping of our adversaries in Vietnam into one personified Enemy—"*He* hopes that by resistance and terror he can do thus and so"—confuses what we are trying to obtain. The coalition against which the United States is engaged in Vietnam includes China, Russia, and North Vietnam under a strained political alliance with people from the South, including hard-core Communists, nationalists, anticolonialists, loyalists, and local politicians interested in their own positions. It is difficult to think of any position which that group, acting together, could take in negotiations. If we required a collective decision in response to our bombing program, there was probably no decision that particular conglomeration of political interests could take except to continue what they had been doing— fighting, resistance, terror. That is, there was *no* decision we would like which they would be capable of making, no matter how the choice looked to them. Even supposing that we were able to draft and present a yesable proposition for a cease-fire or mutual program of de-escalation which would be attractive to some of these groups, others would fall off and continue fighting.

If we had asked ourselves more accurately whom we were trying to influence, we might have attempted to pursue a policy of influencing individual groups which were more inclined to be influenced by us and which were sufficiently cohesive to split off and make a favorable decision. Perhaps district leaders in the South had sufficient command in their village or district to be able to decide to opt out of the war and to accept some kind of local cease-fire agreement. If the only decision we can imagine our adversaries might conceivably make collectively is one which we do not want, we should pursue policies which attempt to influence them separately. Analogous to the military policy of divide and conquer, we should divide so they can decide.

For many purposes a single country is not a unit which reaches a collective decision. As difficult as the task may be, we should try to identify the individuals or group who are in a position to make the decision we want. If we are trying to influence "Rhodesia," we should decide whether it is the existing government we want to make a decision, a group of leading citizens (in which case, can we identify them?), or black-nationalist leadership. And in each case we should ask ourselves what decision it is that those we are trying to influence are capable of making.

Among those capable of making the decision we should select the most promising target. A domestic lobbyist knows that any congressman might introduce some proposed legislation, but he concentrates on the most promising one. Depending on the character of the decision, we may wish to focus on a group or on an individual. Groups are prone *not* to reach certain kinds of decisions. To deter affirmative action or to avoid a change of position we may wish to raise the matter in a group which will be unable to make a choice. An outside government could best influence the United States to continue its policy of nonrecognition of China, for example, by having the matter raised in Congress. Although the nominal power resides in the Executive, a congressional debate could have a substantial and inhibiting effect. If that government wished us to reverse our policy, they might concentrate on having the matter raised privately for presidential decision.

Since the very concept of decision involves some finality, we may be unable to influence those on whom we have been working to change their collective mind. One attempt

at influence having failed, we may wish to identify a different object of influence simply to try somebody different.
Having failed to persuade the Soviet Union to reconvene
the Geneva Conference to deal with Vietnam, the United
States might have tried to select some other influential
neutrals, like the Pope or the Organization of African Unity,
and to develop a comparable decision which they might be
expected to make.

We are interested not only in immediate results but also
in the effect on future disputes which will result from the
technique of influence we pursue. Sometimes there is a good
reason for seeking a decision by the highest authorities. On
the Berlin autoroute the United States at various times dele-
gated responsibility for dealing with local differences to
local personnel. This was done to avoid a heads-of-state
confrontation over every needless delay by a Soviet official
or small infraction by an American soldier. The result, however, was unfortunate. The local official turned out to take
a more provincial view of the problem. He tended to regard
himself as standing at the crucial point in a cold-war confrontation, where any sign of softness would constitute
treason. Experience there suggested that high officials in
Washington and Moscow would be more willing to make
modest concessions to avoid dispute than would the local
corporal on the scene.

Generally speaking, however, our efforts will be less disruptive and more successful if we can identify as the responsible decider a group or official lower in the hierarchy. To
seek a decision of a clerk is less likely to provoke a crisis
than to seek that decision of a prime minister. At lower
levels different officials deal with different problems. The
decision we want is more likely to be dealt with on its merits
by someone who knows the facts and to whom the facts

are important. Political relations are not so vulnerable, since disagreement on one matter is less likely to mean disagreement on another. Further, dealing with a lower official leaves us the chance of appealing to a higher one. This provides scope for two countries to reveal how deeply a matter concerns them, and scope to correct a matter with minimum loss of face. When Professor Frederick Barghoorn of Yale was arrested by Soviet authorities in 1963, the United States might have sought relief from Soviet officials or from the top man. President Kennedy chose to make a personal and public demand of Premier Khrushchev. The effort was successful, but at a cost. If Khrushchev had refused to release Barghoorn despite the President's demand, a major crisis could quickly have erupted.

The occasional difficulties of "meddling" in another country's affairs do not vitiate the general advantages of seeking to exert influence at the lowest level which is capable of reaching the desired decision. Day-to-day cooperation between the Soviet Union and the United States in the conservation of fur-bearing seals in the North Pacific, cooperation which continued throughout the most critical periods of the cold war, succeeded in building the herds up from an estimated 60,000 to over 2 million by 1964. Much of this success is due to the fact that reciprocal requests were sent back and forth between fish-and-wildlife people in the United States and their counterparts in the Soviet Union rather than between those officials in each country who were handling the Berlin and other crises.

Having decided whom we should really try to influence, we face the question of what we ought to say on that subject. There may be advantages in talking as if we were trying to influence someone else. For instance, the true purpose of sanctions against Rhodesia may have been to

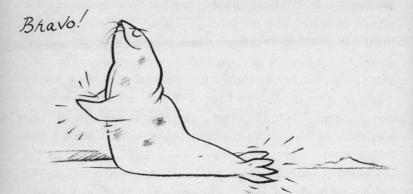

Bravo!

prevent other African countries from taking stronger action against Rhodesia. Although the true purpose of our diplomatic protest may be to seek a high-level decision, we may want to behave as if the right decision had already been made at the highest level of the other government and that only certain lower officers had engaged in unauthorized conduct. Such an approach may make it easier to get the desired decision by allowing the other government to save face. This does not always work smoothly. Although Khrushchev suggested to President Eisenhower that the U-2 overflights of the Soviet Union were no doubt unauthorized activity on the part of the CIA, Eisenhower did not take the easy way out. He first publicly insisted that he personally had authorized the flights, and then publicly reached the high-level decision to stop them.

To identify a particular officer publicly as the decision maker within a foreign government may seriously handicap him. But the advantage of public anonymity should not lead us to conclude that the decider himself need not know he is faced with a decision. He is unlikely to reach a decision unless he knows he has a choice to make. Britain should have done more to identify those leading citizens of Rhodesia who were being asked to indicate a willingness to return to constitutional government. In effect Britain was saying to about three hundred people, "We would like some twenty of you to undertake a hazardous task which could just as well be undertaken by any other twenty among you." No designated group was put in a position in which, if it did not make a decision, none would be made. In such circumstances the tendency to look the other way is enormous. When influencing unidentified members of a larger group it may be better to select some at random than to wait for volunteers. The army sergeant who says, "I want three volunteers: you, you and you," may not get those with the best motivation, but he does get somebody. Similarly, within a government no one officer or department is likely to feel charged with the responsibility of raising a matter for decision unless our policy is designed at least to single them out.

ASK FOR SOMETHING ELSE

As I have suggested, the decision we would like to have an adversary make is not something we can find a priori from examination of the problem, or from asking ourselves what it is that we do not like about the situation. It does not exist in the air. It must be carefully formulated so that those with the power to decide perceive a choice that is open to them and so that we can arrange that the consequences of making that choice appear more favorable to them than the consequences of not making it. The formulation and reformulation of the decision we seek is, I believe, the single most important element in the successful conduct of foreign affairs. In order to escape some of the common errors of formulating a decision and exerting influence, we should at a minimum define our objective so that the other government perceives a choice open to them and so that it is within the realm of the possible that they will make the choice we desire.

Usually an adversary government has little idea of the range of decisions which would be acceptable to us; often, as suggested, they will put the worst possible interpretation on our objectives. Sometimes it is possible to reinterpret what we are asking for by using different words or by emphasizing certain elements. The Potsdam reinterpretation of our demand for the "unconditional surrender" of Japan as a set of specific terms around the unconditional surrender of the military forces not only made our demand much more attractive but also encouraged consideration of the consequences to Japan which would actually result from the Japanese government's making the desired decision. We can also reinterpret our demand in procedural rather than substantive terms. Usually we appear interested in a substantive result. However, substantive results are likely to depend upon factual assumptions—assumptions with which others may disagree. Instead of a government partial to us, we might seek a government freely elected by the people. Having as an objective the reaching of some result by a fair procedure, rather than the reaching of a particular result, usually broadens the acceptability of the demand.

Simply restating our objective in their terms may alter their perception of what we are asking for. At the outset of American involvement in Vietnam our government spoke of our objectives in terms like "teaching the Communists a lesson" and demanding an end of North Vietnamese efforts to take over the South. Later, at various times, United States officials referred to our objective as the implementation of the Geneva Accords of 1954, an objective also nominally adopted by our adversaries. There can be no doubt that to state our objective in such terms would make it easier for others to accept it and hence increase the chances that we would get what we want.

Although ultimately we are not as interested in what another government says as we are in what they do, in the short run our objectives might best be satisfied by getting a promise from them—a decision to say something rather than a decision to act. No matter how much we distrust an adversary or think that it is action we want, we should consider whether we might better be asking them to promise something, offer something, or talk about something. In World War II the immediate objective during the summer of 1945 was to get the Emperor of Japan to *say* he was willing to surrender. The actual laying down of arms by Japan was easier to accomplish once the promise of surrender had been given. The promise was worth more to us than any conduct. If the Emperor had said nothing, gone into retirement, and had nothing more to do with the war, various generals would no doubt have continued fighting. The actual performance of even many members of the group would not have been as valuable as the promise that the institution would perform collectively.

In other cases a promise may be easier to get than an act, but not worth as much. The following list suggests the different qualities of conduct which we may seek from an adversary government. In changing from one to another we are not necessarily abandoning our former objective.

Do what we want you to do.
Stop doing what we don't want you to do.
Make us a promise.
Make us an offer.
Respond to our offer.

Negotiate toward an agreement.
Explain your position.
Describe your position.
Say something.
Don't do something that you are not now doing.

A promise is far better than nothing, and it will make the act more likely; it gives us another tool with which to exert influence. As a standard practice the United States government should try to write out the terms of a promise, such as a draft cease-fire agreement, a draft press statement, or a draft letter, which it could reasonably expect from each government we are trying to influence, such as North Vietnam, Cuba, and France. Thinking in terms of the actual words of a statement or an agreement makes it necessary to think precisely about what we are trying to do. If this effort causes us to lower our sights, our immediate objective might be to seek not a promise, but an offer: some clear indication of the kind of promise or action an adversary would be willing to undertake if something or other should happen. Or we may first try for negotiations or some more rudimentary communication which through mutual education would perhaps lead to negotiations.

Where the legitimacy of one party is in dispute, the fact of negotiations may confer status and be costly to the other. The reluctance of South Vietnam to negotiate with the Vietcong resulted in part from the fear that to do so would have conferred a great deal of the status which the dispute was about. In such circumstances it ought to be possible to arrange to accomplish the mutual education aspect of negotiations without affecting the bargaining aspect. Perhaps this could be done by having a few highly informed officials respected by and sympathetic to the position of one government or the other sit down together and try to work out some drafts of the kind of agreement which negotiations might produce. The results of their discussion should help both sides better understand the position of the other.

Often the easiest type of objective to achieve is to have a government continue to refrain from doing something they are not now doing, and we may wish to change our demand to one of that kind. Differences of view within their government, red tape, and the difficulties of bringing about a change in government policy would all be on our side. There is no need for a government to admit or to indicate that they have been influenced by others; they just continue not to do what they have not been doing.

Another type of objective which is particularly likely to be successful is one which we have the capability to achieve or nearly achieve by self-help. We are more likely to be able to exert influence on an adversary government to make a decision when, if they do not make it, we will be able to go ahead and achieve our aims anyway. There are several reasons for this. Suppose we went to a committee that is building a hospital. Instead of saying it will cost an extra $100,000 to finish the hospital, we say, "We've discovered you are building on quicksand, and there is a 65 per cent chance the building will collapse." Such a warning is likely to be quite influential in producing a decision not to complete the building; the threat of lack of success—the failure of expected benefits—is often more powerful than a threat of high costs. If we say to someone, "Give that to me or I'll step on your toes," he may keep it. If we say, "Give it to me or I'll take it," and we have a demonstrated capacity to take it, he is more likely to comply. In addition, a threat to achieve the objective by self-help is much more credible, since an adversary knows that if he does not make the desired decision, we have a self-interest in carrying out the

threat beyond making our future threats credible. It is a
threat we will want to carry out in order to produce results.
In Thomas Schelling's vocabulary, it is not a threat but a
warning.

WE CAN MAKE THE DEMAND MORE SPECIFIC

The advantages of being ambiguous about the decision
we would like another government to make are often emphasized. Through ambiguity we can avoid confronting our
adversary with something which will look like an ultimatum.
An explicit request, even if privately communicated, involves risks for them. It is within our power to make the
transaction public. If the demand is ambiguous they incur
less political risk in meeting it and are therefore more likely
to go along in the direction suggested. Ambiguity also allows
the other government to meet our general desires in the
manner which is most convenient and least costly to them.
The demand may be easier to go along with if an adversary
can formulate the details himself. At least they can have
the satisfaction of being involved in the process of working
out a compromise consistent with some general formula.
Making a specific request public increases the cost to us
of backing down or compromising, which may often be dis-
advantageous. The demand for international inspection of
Cuba made at the time of the Cuban missile crisis was much
more ambiguous than the demand that the Soviet Union
remove its nuclear missiles. It was far easier for the Soviet
Union to fail to deliver on this request and far easier for
the United States to accept U-2 overflights as a substitute.
Most important, being specific is likely to put a ceiling on
what we can hope to attain. We are unlikely to get anything

more favorable. An adversary is likely to start at that point and try to bargain us down. It is often said that being specific at the outset is just poor bargaining.

The disadvantages of ambiguity in communicating international demands are, however, often greater, and usually go unrecognized. These disadvantages are particularly acute if we are seeking to influence a government to take some affirmative action. Any ambiguity about what we want that government to do makes it that much less likely that they will do it. Influencing another government in a conflict situation is usually far more difficult than negotiating dollars and cents across the bargaining table. Communication about actual decisions we would like another government to make is scarce. The level of hostility is likely to be high. Messages are often misunderstood. A bargaining buyer is involved in a process in which he is predisposed to re-evaluate his position, to change his mind, to dicker. Governments are rarely so disposed. It will simplify their decision-making process if we communicate a clear choice—if we give them a yes-able proposition. One of the difficulties with the way in which foreign policy is presently pursued is that governments too rarely get to a bargaining-table situation. The style is not to communicate actual, practical goals back and forth. Communicating with a great deal of specificity decisions we would like to have other governments make may be the mode of communication to adopt if we wish to exert influence. In many circumstances, it may be the only way to establish effective communication.

Consider the situation in Vietnam, for example, in March of 1965, as it might have looked to the North Vietnamese. At that time the United States was asking North Vietnam to "stop its aggression" in the South and indicating that American bombing of the North would stop as soon as that happened. Probably the ambiguous nature of the demand to "stop aggression" operated to undercut any pressure on North Vietnam to stop its support for the South. First, even those in North Vietnam who wanted to do something which would end the bombing probably put the most pessimistic interpretation on what it would take to satisfy us. Second, having left up to them the selection of an appropriate action which would constitute "stopping aggression," we made it unlikely that they would be able to come to an institutional agreement upon something they would be willing to do. Third, the fact of ambiguity would naturally have deterred them from trying out any action upon which they could agree. They could, perhaps, be certain that the United States would stop the bombing if they, North Vietnam, did everything that could conceivably fall within our definition of aggression: stop all infiltration of men and supplies, recall all "regroupees" born in the South and trained in the North, order them to destroy all equipment already infiltrated, stop all further propaganda and political support for the National Liberation movement, and publicly repudiate the Vietcong program. They could, however, be equally certain that something less than that would be sufficient to get the United States to stop the bombing. But how much less? In taking any particular action, they would risk doing more than we would have regarded as sufficient (paying too high a price) or not doing enough (paying a price and getting nothing for it). Since time was not of utmost importance, the choice of waiting at least one more day for the situation to clarify naturally looked more attractive to them than the choice of paying a price in the dark. It was as though we had offered to sell a horse for "a reasonable sum," the buyer being required to pay his money over the table first: if he paid enough the first time, we would give him the horse; if not, no sale and we would keep the money. A buyer might be confident that he could get the horse for $1,000 and might even be willing to pay that much if he knew he had to, but in such a situation there is no specific sum he will pass over the table. Any amount is either almost certainly too high or runs a great risk of being too little.

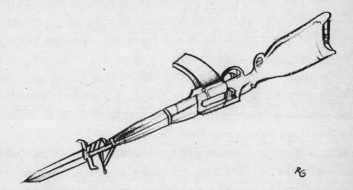

Being ambiguous about the decision we would like may get us nothing at all. By 1966 it appears that we recognized the bind into which we had put the North Vietnamese. So we began to say, "Just do the minimum. Any assurance regarding a willingness to de-escalate would be sufficient to justify our stopping the bombing. Almost any assurance." It would have been instructive had we tried to write out some hypothetical assurances which we could realistically have expected Ho Chi Minh to make if he were interested in having the bombing stop. It turns out that most of the promises he might have made do not look very good. Suppose the North Vietnamese had said, "All right, we'll cut infiltration by 30 per cent. Now stop the bombing." We would have wanted to say, "Hold on, let's clarify this a little. Thirty per cent of what? Last month's infiltration? Next month's planned infiltration? How will we verify this 30 per cent reduction? Will it continue? How long?" Certainly Hanoi would have realized that our reaction to such an assurance would probably be equivocal. Anyone in the inner councils of the North Vietnamese government would have had a hard time convincing the whole Central Committee that all they had to do was say "30 per cent" and the bombing would stop. The apparent generosity of our saying "almost any assurance" was designed to influence spectators, not our adversaries. We did not think through the kinds of specific decisions which North Vietnam would know would be adequate to stop the bombing. President Johnson's broad offer to negotiate with North Vietnam "anywhere at any time" suffered from similar vagueness and proved difficult to convert into an operational decision.

One difficulty of ambiguity is illustrated by the first Security Council cease-fire resolution in the Arab-Israeli war of June, 1967. That resolution called on the parties to take "forthwith" all measures for an "immediate" cease-fire. This was a yesable proposition but one into which a certain amount of ambiguity was inserted to meet a confused situation. It only made the situation more confused. Since individual military units received word of the truce call at different times, for each unit "forthwith" meant something different. Each unit, as it got word of the demand, apparently considered further firing on its positions by others as demonstrating that no cease-fire was taking place and as justifying continued combat operations. Fighting did not stop. (The next Security Council resolution tried to meet this problem by demanding that the governments concerned "discontinue all military activities at 2000 hours GMT on 7 June 1967.") The more specific the arrangements for any cease-fire, the more likely it is to be successful. A cease-fire which specifically contemplated instances of noncompliance

and provided a procedure for dealing with them would reduce the importance of such incidents and reduce the likelihood that when they occurred they would cause widespread fighting to erupt again.

In the present style of conducting foreign policy we too often define our demands generally, giving an adversary a great choice in selecting action in which it could engage to satisfy our demands. ("We hope the Soviet Union will undertake some reciprocal measures which will further reduce tension." "We hope very much to see some response which we have not yet seen on the ground in the direction of de-escalation of the violence.") Seldom do we identify specifically and narrowly some bit of conduct in which we would like them to engage ("remove forty-two weapons from Cuba"). Yet one of the most effective ways of getting action is to come up with a specific, yesable proposition. The easier it is for a government to make a decision, the more likely they are to make it. Also, they are more likely to consider the actual advantages and disadvantages of the choice. Even when we want to produce negotiations rather than affirmative action, it will often be helpful to become more specific: we need not disclose our secret thoughts about a minimum acceptable solution, but negotiations may move forward if the other government has a clearer idea of what would be satisfactory to us.

SPECIFICITY IS NOT RIGIDITY

Becoming specific about decisions which we would like another government to make need not be a bad bargaining technique, nor will it rigidify our position, so long as we communicate more than one proposal. Illustrative specificity can indicate the kind of decision which would satisfy us. It should stimulate their thinking and open lines of communication. It will also indicate that we are searching for a solution and are not tied to one plan. And it will give an adversary several yesable propositions while encouraging them to work out more for themselves. It would have been easy for our government to communicate specific examples of the kind of statement we would have accepted from North Vietnam as a signal that they were willing to "stop aggression." But for years nobody in our government communicated such drafts.

What would a promise look like—one which they might realistically make and which we could accept immediately? They might agree to stop infiltraton through the Demilitarized Zone; cut total infiltration to a third of that of the previous month, with certain specific arrangements for allowing us to verify that they were doing it; promise to end rocket attacks on specific South Vietnamese cities; maintain the existing troop level of troops in the South with a cut-off on infiltration of arms over a certain size or fire power; cut their troop level by a certain number of men. Much earlier we should have been saying, "Here are six things you can do which will produce an end to the bombing. This is the direction in which we are thinking. We need an indication. If these aren't satisfactory, tell us what you might be prepared to do if it were acceptable to us." Such a message would have stimulated discussion and thinking on their side. They would have had more reason to believe we were serious. And the demand would have given them a specific choice to make, since they could have been sure of getting the offer (no more bombing) for making the desired decision.

Illustrative specificity helps avoid the appearance of rigidity which comes from putting forward only one plan. Both before and after President Johnson's letter to Ho Chi Minh in the spring of 1967 there were public statements that there were any number of things we would have accepted. We said that all sorts of possibilities were open. Yet the letter immediately began to be referred to as "the" American position of what the North Vietnamese would have to do: cut off all infiltration of men and supplies and demonstrate that they had done so. We had failed to identify specifically more than one assurance. And bureaucracies tend to see a single illustrative example as a fixed minimum requirement: what should be labeled an example tends to become something we insist upon. In order to avoid this, it is helpful to have two or more suggestions on the table at the same time. This combines flexibility with the advantages of confronting an adversary with a specific choice.

AT LEAST WE SHOULD BE SPECIFIC IN OUR OWN THINKING

There is a difference between being specific in our own minds about the kind of decisions we would like another government to make and communicating those decisions specifically. Although in most cases we would be more successful by being more specific in our communication, circumstances sometimes call for a degree of ambiguity. But no matter how ambiguously we decide to communicate with an adversary, we should internally do the necessary staff work to develop in precise words and phrases some illustrative decisions we would like our adversary to make. We are unlikely to get what we want unless we know what that is. We also need a clear idea of what that decision is in order to arrange the consequences of their making or not making the decision. We ought to understand just what they

do to get the "carrot" and what they do to get the "stick." As the Paris negotiations over Vietnam started, the United States should have had in mind drafts of possible joint communiqués which we would have liked and which we could realistically expect the talks might produce. What might be the wording of acceptable joint statements about the bombings, about reciprocal de-escalation, about negotiations among the South Vietnamese, and about Laos? By being specific internally we get the benefits of clear thinking without committing ourselves to a specific position in public.

There will be opposition to this kind of thinking, of course. It requires the bureaucracy to spend time and effort working out specific examples of what we would accept although they may never be communicated. This process will often engender internal conflict between departments and officials in our own government, with little apparent reward. Working on actual drafts is, however, a useful and an educational experience. Again, it will be useful to develop several specific proposals, this time to avoid internal rigidity. Such work is bound to stimulate our own thinking about what it is we are trying to get our adversary to do; it is just this kind of thinking which my experience suggests has often been absent in policy making.

WE CAN FRACTIONATE THE PROBLEM

When we want another government to stop doing something, we usually have no trouble in identifying the core of the conduct to which we object. The problem is to define for ourselves the amount and kind of objectionable conduct we should try to stop at one time with the means at our disposal. Our federal government objects strongly to racial discrimination that is officially supported or condoned by state governments, and they have a long-term objective of abolishing it completely. In selecting a working objective, however, they have to consider how much of what is going on they can realistically expect to stop within a given period of time. Their effectiveness in stopping any may depend upon not trying to stop too much at one time. The same applies to international objectives. The government of South Vietnam wishes an end to all aggression supported from the North, including the removal from the South of men trained in the North and of equipment brought down from the North, the termination of all radio broadcasts and demonstrations against their government, and so forth. Adopting a more limited objective would increase the chance of attaining it.

We saw that it should be an important part of foreign policy to *formulate* the decisions we want another government to make, even if we do not ask specifically for those decisions. One way to look at the problem of formulating objectives—desired decisions—is in terms of size: how much shall we try for, now? We cannot eliminate a conflict of interest which exists, but by defining the size of a given dispute—what is included and what is not—we can affect it significantly. In August, 1961, a civil aviation agreement between the United States and the Soviet Union was negotiated. The United States might have signed the agreement, treating it as a separate matter. We chose to treat it as part of the then pending Berlin confrontation and refused to sign. In 1968 both the United States and the U.S.S.R. were prepared to treat the New York–Moscow air route as unrelated to Berlin or to Vietnam, to sign the agreement, and to put it into effect.

After Brazil expropriated an American-owned telephone

company in 1962, there were suggestions in Congress that because of this fundamental dispute between Latin America and the United States we should give no further aid to the Alliance for Progress. The President at a press conference, however, defined the dispute as one between the governor of a province and a single American company over the form and amount of compensation due. In 1964, the New York World's Fair Committee asked the White House whether the Peking government should be invited to exhibit at the fair. A White House decision that the Peking government should not be invited turned a nongovernmental issue into a governmental one. The issue would have been downgraded had either the committee or the White House decided that the matter was for the committee to decide.

To be effective in domestic politics one often tries to combine the public support which broad issues can arouse with the pursuit of narrowly defined goals. In attempting to influence another government, it is equally important to define the immediate goal narrowly, to break up a big issue into smaller ones, and to press for these separately. This technique has been called "salami tactics"—moving ahead one thin slice at a time. Where a confrontation involves big issues, we should not ask ourselves what kind of a final outcome we would like if everybody did what we would like him to do. We should instead ask ourselves exactly what we would like to have happen next.

In any conflict we should consider changing the situation through dividing up the issues and specifying the distinct things we would like our adversary to decide. For example, the following is a list which could have served for at least half a dozen years as a list of things we might like to have happen in Cuba

—with respect to the Soviet Union:

> 1. withdrawal of all Soviet military personnel
> 2. no base for Soviet submarine or military "trawlers"

—with respect to Latin America:

> 3. no shipment of arms from Cuba
> 4. no training for export of militant revolutionaries
> 5. some form of OAS inspection of a nuclear-free Latin America

—with respect to the United States:

> 6. some steps toward compensation of property taken by Castro
> 7. acceptance by Cuba of general international obligations

—inside Cuba:

> 8. free speech and other civil liberties
> 9. elections
> 10. public assertion of an independent ideology, drawing, say, from Jefferson and Lincoln as well as Marx and Lenin

When we really wanted to exert influence on Cuba, we defined the issues even more narrowly. In the latter part of October, 1962, we were keenly interested in the removal from Cuba of particular Soviet weapons. We prudently stopped talking about ousting Communism from the Western Hemisphere and concentrated on the removal of forty-two weapons. When we wanted to obtain freedom for the prisoners captured at the Bay of Pigs, we separated that aim from other outstanding issues and bargained with food and medicine. When we and the Soviet Union become serious about the arms race, we stop demanding complete and general disarmament and get to work on specific proposals to limit particular arms.

In most cases a government increases its chances of getting something by asking for less. Since it will be easier to take the first step, there is greater likelihood of getting something rather than nothing. This is the strategy of the camel who concentrated first on getting his nose inside the tent. Setting a limited objective may also make future success in resolving the bigger issue more likely. Although some people may think the whole issue has been resolved, one success at influence may set a psychological background for bigger demands. More important, splitting the issues asks our adversary to consider each issue on its merits rather than in a broad ideological scheme. We should attempt to avoid publicly setting each issue which is capable of separate resolution in the framework of some over-all political confrontation. The over-all confrontation may be a correct diagnosis; one step at a time may still be the best prescription.

If we continue in the United Nations and elsewhere to press for many separate objectives—particularly if our position makes practical sense—we will have a fair chance of getting them. If the objectives are small, no one defeat will cause any country to pick up its chips and go home. Separating objectives into their smallest components and dealing with them separately will also reduce the risk of war. No country is likely to fight over what it perceives as a small issue. When the decision we demand is a small one, it is likely to be more yesable and receive more pointed consideration. Dividing up a problem makes it possible for countries to agree on issues on which they have common interests, limiting disagreement to those issues on which they truly disagree. This was certainly true of the partial test-ban treaty. Unable to agree on large issues, we made an effective agreement on what we *could* agree on. This treaty probably helped rather than hindered the negotiation of further agreements.

Changing the choice with which an adversary is confronted by focusing on a narrower part of the decision we are asking them to make is a good technique for another important reason. We saw the inherently ambiguous nature of a decision to proceed in the face of possible risks: such a decision is often interpreted as a decision to see a course of action through to the end regardless of the risks that materialize. Thus reaching agreement on the first steps of a temporary cease-fire may, by starting an adversary off in a given direction, make it difficult to resume fighting.

In some cases the disadvantages of breaking up a large issue will outweigh the advantages. A bargain must be big enough to have something in it for each side. But in all cases it is wise for a government to adopt an objective with a conscious awareness of the possibilities of making it smaller or larger.

WE SHOULD NOT ALWAYS ASK FOR MORE THAN WE EXPECT

Governments regularly ask for more than they can reasonably expect to get. That fact alone tends to set a style for intergovernmental negotiations—a style that cannot be ignored. There are some obvious advantages to "padding" a demand. If we get anything at all, we are likely to get more than we would have got without padding. We have room to retreat, and at the same time it will seem more politically acceptable and more profitable for an adversary to accept a demand which is lower than our initial one. So we seem more likely to get our "real" price. Also it is easier for the public to judge whether or not we have been successful by the change our adversary has made from his initial position than by the substance of what we got in the end: therefore, padding may make it easier for each side to marshal public support for a compromise.

However, if we add too much to the price, we may scare off the customers: they will not even be interested in talking. President Johnson's letter to Ho Chi Minh in the spring of 1967 suffered from too much padding. It was meant as an opening gambit. Although we said, "We will stop the bombing if you stop all infiltration and demonstrate that you've done so," we also meant "and if this is not satisfactory, what will you do?" This was an offer on our part to promise not to increase our troop levels in exchange for a demonstration on their part that they had abandoned their troops and left them without supplies or replacements. This was a specific, yesable proposition, but it was so well padded that it elicited no interest. The fact that Ho Chi Minh published it to the world to gain a propaganda advantage indicates that, in his eyes at least, the world would not rate this proposal as that of a government sincerely seeking some mutually satisfactory arrangement. The padding scared the customer away. No negotiations took place for a year, during which time thousands of Americans were killed. A more realistic proposal might have been to our advantage.

There are two reasons for setting a high price on goods. One is that the seller realistically hopes the buyer will pay that price: he weighs the risk of not making the sale against the advantage of getting more money if he does make the sale. That is not true padding. Padding is the setting of a phony high price in the hope that the customer will be more willing to buy once the price has been marked down. It is not always appreciated that the "bargaining" argument for starting with a high price applies only to a situation where the seller is seeking negotiations rather than performance. Although the stated demand may be for the payment of a given price, the true objective is an expression of interest on the part of the buyer—negotiations. Where negotiations are not wanted (for example where the sale is being made by a vending machine), it is obvious that to state an artificially high price is self-defeating. If our object is to make a donkey jump over a fence, it does not help to put an extra bar on the fence for negotiating purposes. The best technique is to make the hurdle minimally difficult in the first instance.

Padding often results in our maintaining a position which is politically weak. Our adversary, rather than entering into negotiations, may concentrate on subjecting us to a propaganda attack to which we have made ourselves vulnerable. We may suffer a political cost in third countries for insisting on an unrealistic demand: Britain's insistence on unconditional surrender from Ian Smith in Rhodesia (not even offering him immunity from prosecution for treason) pleased some African countries in the short run, but Britain then began to pay high long-run costs for that exaggerated demand.

Domestically, we risk tying our own hands. In a situation in which the public has no previously formed view about a proper outcome, its government's first demand sets an objective. As that demand is repeated, it tends to become increasingly difficult for the government to draw back from it. What starts out as fat may end up as bone. In the unsuccessful negotiations for a ban on underground testing of nuclear weapons, the United States publicly adopted the

position that a satisfactory treaty would require that each major nuclear power be given a quota of at least seven inspection trips every year. No one knew what constituted an inspection: how many men could visit how large an area for how long a time. But the number "seven" took on a political life of its own. Senators and columnists argued that the United States could not retreat from seven to three. Whatever the merits of the position, it was clear that by starting out at one point identifiable in numerical terms the government had created strong domestic resistance to their shifting to a lower point.

Padding may also be positively harmful. Once we begin to retreat from a padded position, we begin to acquire a reputation for retreating. An adversary might reasonably conclude that if we came down once, we will come down again. They may not believe us when we say that we have come to the end of the padding.

CONCLUSION

These are a few examples of ways in which we can change what we are asking for in an effort to increase our chance of exerting influence—our chance of getting another government to make a decision which we want them to make. They are not exclusive. They suggest that we ought to be spending more time examining just what it is we are asking them to do, and less time repeating what we are going to do to them if they don't do it.

5

Improve What Happens to Them if They Are Good

GOVERNMENTS necessarily consider the consequences of their decisions. They compare, crudely or carefully, the expected results of making a given decision with the expected results of not making it. The standard way of exerting influence on other governments is to try to alter their perception of some of these expected results. For any given decision, two sets of results are involved, one for making it and one for not making it.

In each set of results some are likely to be favorable to the government and some unfavorable. The effective pressure upon a government to decide one way or the other depends upon the difference between the perceived net "pay-off" of making the decision weighed against the perceived net "pay-off" of not doing so. Although these pay-offs are almost never subject to quantitative valuation, it is useful to try to sketch out to the best of our ability a hypothetical balance sheet as it might be prepared by the government we are trying to influence.

As an example, consider the choice facing the government of North Korea in February, 1968, after they had seized the United States Navy's electronic reconnaissance vessel *Pueblo* and its crew in waters off the coast of North Korea. The United States government, insisting that the ship had been illegally seized on the high seas, demanded the immediate return of the ship and the crew. To the government of North Korea the choice presented in terms of a balance sheet may have looked something like the following:

I. NORTH KOREA'S CHOICE JUST AFTER THE PUEBLO WAS SEIZED
("we" = North Korea)

If we return the ship and crew	If we keep the ship and crew
(+) Almost no risk of military reprisal.	(−) Some risk of military reprisal.
(−) We admit the seizure was wrong.	(+) We gain intelligence from ship and crew.
We yield to U.S. military blackmail.	We show U.S. to be powerless.
We look incompetent.	We divert U.S. from Vietnam.
We accept the legitimacy of spyboats.	We support war against U.S.
	We intimidate South Korea.
	We tend to split South Korea from U.S.
	We direct attention to U.S. spying.
	We can always return ship and crew later.

If that is anything like a fair estimate of the choice as it looked to the government of North Korea, it is not surprising that the ship was kept despite the United States demand for its return. The left-hand column constitutes what we have been calling the offer—the consequences that result from making the desired decision. From the North Korean point of view it was not an attractive offer. The right-hand column constitutes what we have been calling the threat, yet from the North Korean point of view it looked pretty attractive.

The normal first reaction is to try to exert influence by making the threat side less attractive. In the *Pueblo* case the United States sent naval ships toward Korea in a "show of force," endeavoring to increase North Korea's fear of military reprisals should they keep the ship and crew. But this was a difficult task. North Korea was not relying on the lack of United States military capability in the area to prevent military reprisals; they were relying on the fact that they held the crew as hostages. The North Korean government had undoubtedly assessed the risk of our retaliation before they seized the *Pueblo*, and there was little that the hasty movement of United States naval vessels in the area would do to change that risk.

As suggested, a well-considered program for trying to exert influence on North Korea would look at the whole balance sheet as it appeared to the North Koreans and consider what might be done to change the decision we were seeking and to change the consequences which they might expect to follow from making or not making that decision. In such an analysis the possible changes on the offer side of the balance sheet usually hold out greater unexplored opportunities for influence than those on the threat side. This chapter examines ways of exerting influence by making it appear more attractive to another government to do what we would like them to do. Before turning to the general problem, let us consider what might have been done in the case of the *Pueblo*.

The analytical task is to construct a hypothetical or target balance sheet with which we would like to see the North Koreans confronted and a program for getting there. This target balance sheet should be one which we think might cause North Korea to make the decision we would like them to make. Finally, we should sketch out a separate balance sheet for ourselves and determine whether the potential benefit to us of trying to exert this influence is worth the costs.

The approach is illustrated by the following suggestions, which were prepared just after the *Pueblo* was seized:

II. PROGRAM: A POSSIBLE SCHEME DESIGNED TO INFLUENCE NORTH KOREA

Change the demand:

—Suggest that the crew be returned without prejudice to North Korea's position and that the disposition of the ship await a full settlement of the dispute.

Change the threat:

—Remove any threat of immediate military attack by words and by withdrawing U.S. naval ships from the area.

—Identify the threat as being that if the dispute continues the U.S. is likely to embark on a long-term program of building up the military strength of South Korea.

Change the offer:

—Recognize the incident as one involving issues of fact and law with something to be said for each side.

—Treat the dispute as one of many to be settled peacefully.

—Play down urgency.

—Indicate a willingness to apologize for any intrusion that did occur.

—Promise to discipline any officers if we find that an intrusion into North Korea's waters, whether deliberate or careless, did take place.

—Offer to discuss the general problem of reducing conduct regarded by either side as unduly provocative, including possible limitations on electronic surveillance.

The hope would be that for the United States to pursue such a program would, in a few weeks, confront the North Korean government with a choice which looked quite different from the one they faced when they decided not to return the ship and crew immediately upon the demand of the United States. It might then appear to be roughly as follows:

III. TARGET BALANCE SHEET
NORTH KOREA'S CHOICE AFTER OUR PROGRAM
("we" = North Korea)

If we return the crew

(+) No risk of military reprisal.

We look generous (men are being returned by agreement, not under threat).

Our seizure has been partially vindicated.

We can keep the ship with some legitimacy.

We already have all the intelligence data we can get from the crew.

U.S. accepts some responsibility.

U.S. spyship provocations are less likely in the future.

(—) We may look soft.

We give up hostages which might be a future bargaining counter.

If we keep the crew

(—) An increased risk of U.S.–South Korean build-up.

Increased risk of close cooperation between U.S. and South Korea.

We risk justifying increased U.S. overflights, etc.

We risk criticism from U.S.S.R., Poland, and neutrals.

(+) We maintain our stance as a tough David standing up to Goliath.

We can always return the crew later.

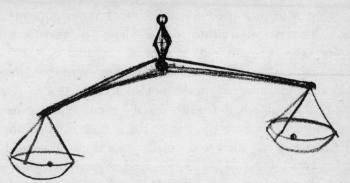

If we could confront North Korea with such a choice we might reasonably expect them to decide to return the crew. Before concluding that we should initiate such a program, however, we would have to strike our own balance sheet and consider the pros and cons, along the following lines:

IV. OUR CHOICE: SHOULD WE ADOPT THE SUGGESTED PROGRAM?
("we" = the U.S.)

If we follow the proposed program

(+) There is a good chance the crew will be returned and the dispute settled peacefully.

If not, we will at least appear reasonable to many people.

(—) We may look soft to the world.

We probably give up any chance of getting the ship back.

In substance, we let North Korea "get away with it."

South Korea may get upset.

We will have to be more careful of our reconnaissance ships in the future.

If we do not

(—) The crew will probably remain in North Korea indefinitely.

The dispute is likely to use up a good deal of time and effort.

The dispute might flare up (but we can probably prevent that).

Some domestic pressure will exist for the government to escalate the dispute.

(+) We do not have to make any decisions now.

We can always do something later if we decide to.

Faced with such a choice, the United States government could have decided either way. Perhaps the fate of some eighty crewmen was not so crucial, considering the rate of casualties being suffered in Vietnam, and the United States could have concluded not to initiate this program designed to obtain the return of the men. What is being argued here is not the wisdom of the suggested program, or that it would have led to a quicker return of the crew, but rather two things: (1) that this kind of analysis helps one think clearly about such a problem, and (2) that a government's choice can be radically and often easily affected by actions designed to change the "offer"—the consequences to them of doing what we want them to do.

Further, it is *not* being suggested that such an analysis is a substitute for detailed knowledge or historical understanding of the people concerned. Quite the contrary. As is apparent from the example, the form of analysis directs attention to questions of national attitude and interest which are likely to affect a government's decision and should help formulate those questions in a way which will make it easier for experts to be of help to decision makers.

The balance of this chapter considers ways of "sweetening the carrot." This is an important way of exerting influence on which there has been far too little organized consideration. In this era of nuclear weapons and deterrence the Department of Defense has become quite sophisticated about making threats. We have no comparable sophistication regarding the making of offers. This is true despite the fact that the process of exerting influence through offers is far more conducive to international peace than the process of exerting influence through threats.

CHANGE THE BENEFICIARY

One way to improve the impact of an offer is to focus on the beneficiary of the offer and his relationship to those we are asking to make the decision. We may be able to improve the effectiveness of the offer by changing those upon whom it has its primary impact. It may be possible, for example, to have the beneficial consequences of a decision fall on those who are more closely involved in the decision. The offer to all Rhodesians of "free participation in a political democracy" if they would return to constitutional government was not much of an offer to those who had the power to make a decision, the Ian Smith government. They were not going to be better off in terms of power. An offer addressed to them should probably have dealt with ways of lessening their fear of a takeover in the near future by an illiterate black majority. When we have identified those to whom the offer is being made, we want to be sure that it appeals to them.

Typically a government making a gesture of friendship looks first to their domestic constituency. Does what we are promising our adversary sound good at home? We also test the offer by the reactions of spectators—international third parties. Does this offer sound generous to others? Only occasionally does it seem important that the consequences of a desired decision should be attractive to those we are trying to influence. The normal tendency is to treat the offer part of the map as window dressing for domestic consumption. We measure our offer in terms of our own values or those of neutrals rather than by the values of the adversary. But the offer will not exert influence unless it appeals to those we are asking to make a decision. They are the ones whose reaction counts most. It is just as important to identify clearly those we are attempting to reward as it is to identify those we are trying to threaten. The best way to have influenced Rhodesia might have been to identify a different group of people in Rhodesia to whom it was possible to make some sort of an offer, to whom Britain could have promised positions in government and power they did not already have in exchange for opposition to the rebellious government.

MAKE THE OFFER MORE ATTRACTIVE

The primary way to improve our offers is to make them look better to the government we are trying to influence. I have used the word "offer" to designate the entire set of consequences to the adversary government of making the decision we want them to make. As we have seen, there are costs as well as benefits to them in this set; there are minuses as well as pluses in the offer. They will presumably be losing some things by changing their minds and making the decision we want them to make. As the example about North Korea showed, we can change the substance of the offer both by improving the advantages they see in making the decision and by reducing or alleviating some of the costs to them of going along with us, costs which also fall on the offer side of the balance sheet.

It is important that there be some pluses. If little thought is usually given to the way an adversary looks at the decision we are asking him to make, even less is given to the attractiveness in his eyes of making it. The fact that we think, "Going along with us on this is a pretty good deal for them; they don't lose much," does not mean that they look at it the same way. An adversary government may not find the consequences of making the desired decision as attractive for them as we do. We should be sure that if we foresee an advantage to them of going along with us, they will be attracted by this advantage and really see it as a plus.

In April, 1965, the United States offered $1 billion in aid to both Vietnams if peace could be restored. But the idea of a $1 billion United States aid program may not have seemed attractive to the North Vietnamese. Political leaders who saw themselves as risking their lives to further national independence, socialism, and anticolonialism may have regarded the prospect of extensive and indefinite economic involvement by a capitalist country in the affairs of Vietnam as more of a threat than a promise. By using their terms and their language and by changing the style of this offer, we might have made it much more attractive to them. We could, for example, have turned $1 billion over to the Asian Development Bank to be used for reconstruction and development in all of Vietnam, it being understood that North Vietnam, if they wished, could consider their share as compensation for damage done by American bombers and artillery fire. The entire program could have been set up to be administered by Asians. Such a scheme would have been far more attractive to North Vietnam and therefore would have exerted, for the same dollar price, far more influence.

This example demonstrates that if we are going to offer the donkey some turnips we had better be sure he likes turnips. We need to have at least some perception of an adversary's values. We ought not to assume that they are a mirror image of ourselves, oriented to the things we would like in the circumstances. What an adversary government likes may not appear to be rational. We may think they are exceptionally foolish. But the more irrational our adversary appears to be, the more important it is that we do not act instinctively but instead act only after we understand how they see the problem and what it is that appeals to them.

We frequently dismiss gestures which we could offer without great cost to ourselves because they are "unimportant." The United States for a long time said that adequate representation of the views of the National Liberation Front in any Vietnam negotiations would be easy to arrange somehow. "There will be no difficulty about that. It really isn't all that important." It may not have been important to us, but it was probably quite important to them. Israel indicated that it was not important to allow United Nations troops on their side of the border as well as on the Egyptian side to show that the arrangement was not discriminatory. It was unimportant to allow UN troops on their soil, even on a narrow strip. It was trivial. Why should they do something which was really unimportant? It was not central to the whole controversy at all. However, the Egyptians took a rather different view of the problem. To them it *was* important. Thinking which does not take the views of another government into consideration is not likely to formulate a decision and its results in a way which will be attractive enough to that government to cause them to make that decision.

REDUCE THE DISADVANTAGES OF MAKING THE DECISION

Perhaps more important to the adversary are the minuses in the offer: the disadvantages to them of going along with the decision we want. One way to improve the offer is to lessen the costs the adversary will incur in making our decision. It is not sympathy for an adversary, but common sense, that says we should make it as easy and attractive as possible for them to do what we would like them to do.

A government is often deterred from making the decision we want by the high political costs they anticipate. Where there are costs in continuing their present course but also costs in changing their minds, inertia may cause them to exaggerate the effect of the costs of change. The *Pueblo* example given above suggests the desirability of working out all the reasons another government may have for not deciding the way we would like them to decide, and of then seeing what we can do to minimize those costs.

In particular, governments are often concerned with the bad precedent which they fear that a particular action will establish. It may be important to reduce the precedential effect of the decision we seek. Consider the case of the Nagas, a people who live in the border region between India and Burma, many of whom wish to have Nagaland recognized as being independent of India. The value of the Naga region to India is probably minimal. It is small and has been difficult to govern. The actual cost of permitting independence there, or at least recognizing some kind of local autonomy, is perhaps negligible. But the political costs of allowing independence to one small part of India, a country in which many geographical areas have strong separatist tendencies, is enormous. One seeking to influence the Indian central government to accept self-government for Nagaland would seek to distinguish its particular case sharply and clearly from the cases of other areas of India. One could reduce this cost by presenting India with a case which relied on unique historical facts applicable only to Nagaland and which avoided arguments based on language or similar considerations available to other Indian states.

In arguing the rightness of a cause we often justify our demand in terms of the broadest possible principles. Presented in this way, our demand will often be hard to accept.

Our adversary cannot accept the case without accepting the principle. If we identify something as a special case—either by distinguishing the issue involved or by channeling the proposed solution through a particular procedural course which will distinguish it from other cases which may arise in the future—we can reduce the scope and effect of the harmful precedent which the other government may fear will be established.

Saving face is important to governments, and this is generally recognized. But arranging the consequences of a decision so that they will be more attractive to the government we are trying to influence involves a great deal more than saving face. "Saving face" implies that what a government is concerned with is superficial appearances rather than substance. Appearances are often important, but limiting the scope of a precedent is not superficial. Nor are many of the other variables which can be changed to make a proposed decision less painful and more appealing to another government. Arranging matters to minimize political costs to an adversary is not window dressing to be put on after the adversary has been persuaded. It is part of the process of persuasion.

MAKE OUR OFFERS MORE CREDIBLE

In addition to changing the substance or content of an offer, we can exert influence by making it appear more likely that what we say will happen will in fact happen. There is necessarily some element of uncertainty in any statement about the future. To the extent that we are seeking to exert influence by holding out attractive consequences for a government if they should make the decision we want

them to make, the more certain we can make those consequences the more successful we will be. We will increase
the impact of our offers if we make them more credible.

Much of our national defense budget has been devoted
to the problem of making our threats credible. We have
spent billions of dollars on nuclear weapons for the sole
purpose of convincing other governments that we have both
the capability and the intention of implementing a threat
of nuclear retaliation. There is a voluminous literature on
threats. The distinction has been explored between threats
narrowly defined and "warnings," consequences which will
result naturally or which we will be compelled by self-
interest to impose and which are therefore more credible.

On the other hand, little attention has been devoted to
the problem of making our offers credible, the problem of
convincing another government that the alleged advantages
of their making a decision we would like them to make will
really materialize. Government officials and critics ought to
pay more attention to this element of policy if only because
it has been so neglected. Moreover, the credibility of offers
may be even more critical than the credibility of threats.

For one thing, even a small chance of having to pay a
great cost is an adequate basis for a governmental decision,
whereas a small chance of a fairly large benefit is not. A
threat may be effective even though it is not highly probable that it would be implemented. It is easy for a political
leader to justify to his government and his own domestic
audience taking a course of action because there was a
20 or 30 per cent chance that, if he did not, the country
would be heavily bombed. A country can be deterred from
doing something by a small risk of disaster. The consequences of the course of action that was avoided remain
uncertain. No one knows for sure what would have hap-

pened. This uncertainty protects the government, which can easily defend their decision to avoid the risk.

Political leaders are not, however, prone to take action on a small chance—a bet—that it will produce very good consequences. Ho Chi Minh might have believed that if

the North Vietnamese stopped fighting and withdrew there was a small chance, but a good one, of a highly favorable outcome: the United States would honor their promise to withdraw completely within six months. But no matter how favorable the outcome, so long as the chance of it appeared small, it would be politically indefensible for him to take that chance. He would not be able to go back to his people and say, "We accepted the American promise because we figured there was a 30 per cent chance we could get what we wanted at no further cost. It was a sound bet under the circumstances. It was a worthwhile risk to take. It just didn't go our way." A government wants to be highly certain that if they make a decision in order to derive some benefits, those benefits are going to materialize.

Unlike the case of a threat which succeeds, here the public has a chance to see what happens. Instead of avoiding uncertainty, and being able to say that no one knows for sure what would have happened, the government has chosen uncertainty. That they gambled and lost is clear for all to see. Although logic would say that in many cases a government ought to decide to pursue a small chance of a high return, the probability that a government will be in the position of having gambled and lost makes this unattractive politically. This is particularly true in an international conflict situation where they will have relied upon the offer or promise of a foreign government. To be effective, offers must be more credible than threats. An offer which is not highly credible will not exert much influence.

Another reason why it is important to make offers credible is that we want to get the maximum influence out of a given offer. To do so we must convince an adversary that we are committed to an offer at least to the extent to which we regard ourselves as committed. If we offer free elections or troop withdrawal within six months, and believe that we are committed to those offers, we are willing to pay such costs for their making the decision we want. Unless we convince them of our degree of commitment, our decision to pay a given cost will have been made in vain. We should make them believe their future is going to be as attractive to them as we believe it's going to be. Since we are making the offer for the purpose of producing an impact, we ought to do all we can to get that impact. Foreign governments are not usually as convinced as we that we are committed to doing what we say we will do. If we are 90 per cent sure we will be willing to pay off if they make the desired decision, then we should attempt to convince them that we are committed at least to that extent. To improve the credibility of a given offer is a far more economical way of exerting influence than to improve the content or generosity of the offer. It is often as though we were offering a seller a check for $100, but the seller is reluctant to let us have the goods because he fears that the check will bounce, that it will not be honored when presented. One way to try to influence the seller in such a case is to increase the amount of the check until he is persuaded to take the chance. A far less costly way, assuming we intend to keep our promise, is to improve the credibility of the check, by establishing our good credit, by getting the check certified by a bank, by putting money in escrow, or by some other such device. Similarly, in political negotiations it will usually be more economical to remove doubts about the genuineness or sincerity of an offer than to try to exert influence by improving the content of an offer about which such doubts exist.

Improving the credibility of a given offer is also likely to be a lower-cost way of exerting influence than to improve the credibility of our threats. If our adversary does not believe that we are as committed to an offer we are presently making as we think we are, a small expense in making that offer more credible may get much more "influence mileage" out of it. What we say and the kinds of arrangements we make can make offers more credible. To make a military threat more credible we may have to spend a great deal on military apparatus which will never be used. The entire out-of-pocket cost is necessary just to demonstrate a capacity to do something we do not want to do. On the other hand little expense should be needed to take preliminary steps which would demonstrate that we are getting ready to carry out an offer.

And increasing the credibility of offers is safer. There is less chance that tension will rise or that the scope of a conflict will be increased. Increasing the likelihood that a given offer will be implemented produces no crisis should the attempt to exert influence fail, produces no animosity, and often provides an acceptable basis for the other government's changing their mind. In contrast, efforts to increase the likelihood that a threat will be implemented tend to produce counterthreats, to increase the risk of disaster should the attempt to exert influence fail, to augment animosity, and to fail to provide an acceptable justification to the other government for changing their mind.

SOME WAYS TO MAKE OUR OFFERS CREDIBLE

One way to increase the perceived probability of our implementing an offer is to increase the actual probability. By making a commitment from which we cannot back down we can show an adversary that we will have to come through on the offer. Even if the North Vietnamese believed that President Johnson was personally committed to the offer of $1 billion in aid, they probably correctly believed that a different administration would feel less bound. They might have thought the offer incredible because it would be difficult to get it through Congress in the event of peace. If we had actually appropriated the money and given it to the Asian Development Bank for distribution when peace was established (perhaps with the interest to be paid to us in the interim), it would not only have been more attractive because of Asian administration; it would also have been far more credible. North Vietnam would have known that if peace came, we could not prevent the implementation of the offer. By committing ourselves, we would have exerted more influence.

Specificity increases the credibility of an offer. For one thing, a specific offer shows that we have thought about what we would be prepared to do and have worked out the details. It is a demonstration of our present intentions. Greater specificity also demonstrates greater commitment and therefore makes for greater credibility. The political cost to us of backing out of a specific promise is greater than that of backing out of a loose or ambiguous one. The more explicit the promise, the more difficult it is to find excuses for nonperformance. By being specific, we buy influence at the cost of flexibility.

A general offer to make sure that the rights of a white minority in Rhodesia are protected does not carry as much weight as a draft treaty or a specific constitution that the government of Great Britain would be willing to sign. An offer to pay a specific sum of money on a particular day carries much more conviction than an offer to pay a fair amount at an appropriate time. On Vietnam President Johnson contributed to the credibility of his offers by being more specific than he might have been. The words "$1 billion" added credibility to an offer of economic assistance after the war. It increased the credibility of our statement that if peace could be restored United States troops would be withdrawn to say we would get out in six months. Not only does "six months" show we have thought about our offer, it shows we are more committed. It becomes more costly politically for the United States to fail to produce on that offer. Therefore, it is more credible and exerts more influence. An offer to withdraw our troops "in due course" would not exert much influence.

Another way to improve the credibility of an offer is to show the adversary that we have detailed plans for implementing it. This factor is more striking the other way around: a lack of detailed planning makes an offer look incredible. The absence of an effort on our part to prepare to implement an offer usually demonstrates that we ourselves do not take it seriously. On the other hand, if an adversary knows that we have contingent plans for carrying out an offer, that we have actually thought about what we are going to do and how we are going to do it, he will be more likely to believe that the offer is serious. Part of our offer to North Vietnam—one of the consequences which we promised if the fighting stopped—was to hold free elections under a strengthened International Control Commission. But how was the commission going to be strengthened? We revealed no proposal for that—not even a rough draft. The commission was weak. They had only one airplane. The notion that it was going to become strong and capable of supervising free elections was incredible in large part because the United States had suggested no plans for strengthening it. Free elections would involve international observers. The lack of detailed planning undercut the prediction, or the promise, that internationally observed elections were ever going to take place. Detail, as both news reporters and confidence men know, is important in lending credibility. Ko-Ko, Lord High Executioner in *The Mikado*, lends plausibility to the description of an otherwise somewhat unbelievable execution scene, by corroborative detail: the look in the man's eye and so on. Contingency plans can supply this corroborative detail. There was no reason for not drawing up further plans for a Vietnam aid program. Terms of fair elections could have been drafted, and plans made for enlarging the control commission, funding it, and recruiting new staff. At small expense, election observers from neutral countries could have been trained. The whole arrangement could have been put on a stand-by basis for instant use when and if needed.

Contingency plans lend credibility to our offers not only because they indicate something about our present intentions, but also because they demonstrate a present capability. An offer will exert little influence if the adversary cannot see how we would be able to implement it. Even if they believe that we are fairly serious about our offer and that we will not look for a way out if they make the decision we are asking them to make, the offer will not exert influence if we appear unable to follow through. Demonstrated capability is just as important with offers as with threats. The white minority of Rhodesia do not perceive the capability on the part of Britain to guarantee white rights should democratic majority government be instituted. One of the things Britain has been offering them is a society in which their freedoms will be protected. But they may see no way in which Britain could protect them from the black majority. Similarly, part of Britain's offer for a return to constitutional government is to call off economic sanctions.

However, mandatory sanctions have now been voted by the United Nations Security Council. Britain can no longer demonstrate even the political capability of officially ending them.

Visible contingency planning for carrying out our offers would involve administrative work, but modest cost. It may well be argued that such efforts would represent a substantial effort to prepare for a situation which may never arise. That is true. But it is equally true that far greater expenditures and efforts are regularly made for military capability which is never used. We have come to recognize that substantial effort is justified in demonstrating our capacity to inflict pain, because that capacity exerts influence. It would be equally worth while to develop and demonstrate a capacity to carry out our offers, particularly when it could be done at a fraction of the cost.

Another way to make our offers credible is to keep our reputation high. A great deal is said about the importance of implementing our threats in order to preserve the credibility of later threats. Yet there is little if any discussion of what happens to our credibility when we fail to implement an offer. If we convince an adversary government that the benefits to them of making a decision we want them to make will be greater than we really think they will be, we improve our chances of successfully exerting influence. But the short-term advantage in influence is likely to be outweighed by the loss of confidence in our future promises. The consequences of a broken promise are serious enough even if the promise was intended to be kept at the time it was made. If the adversary discovers that we never had any intention of keeping the promise—that there was deliberate deception—then our ability to exert influence will be seriously weakened for an indefinite future. As a general rule, it is wise to promise only what we have the capability to deliver.

It is costly to bluff. Bluffing about an offer is more damaging than bluffing about a threat. It is easier to re-establish a reputation for carrying out threats. Any failure to exert influence by a threat can be followed by action demonstrating that this time the threat was not a bluff. If we fail to implement one threat, we can always implement one later. Also, bluffing on one threat may not lead an adversary to conclude we will bluff again. Backing down on the implementation of one threat may, in fact, make it less likely that we will fail to implement a later threat. One could argue that because the Soviet Union "backed down" when faced with a United States quarantine of Cuba, they destroyed their credibility and that the United States could safely ignore any threats the Soviet Union might make about their response if the United States should try to impose a comparable quarantine on the North Vietnamese port of Haiphong. One could make the argument, but it is not convincing. The Soviet ability to make a credible threat may even have been strengthened by their prior yielding. They can now say, and we may believe them, that having backed down once they cannot afford to back down a second time. It is not easy to re-establish a reputation for honoring one's promises. Having been caught bluffing and having acquired a reputation for broken promises, we may not get opportunities to demonstrate that we are now sincere. If we go into a store and say, "I gave you a bad check last week but this one is good," the proprietor may not give us the opportunity to prove we are right.

GIVE THEM THE BENEFITS SOONER

Governments are concerned about the time when the consequences of making a decision are going to materialize. Changing the timing of an offer may be an important way to exert influence. Governments are notoriously shortsighted; they apply a high discount rate. They are much more interested in what is going to happen next week than in what is going to happen next year. The more quickly they can expect the benefits of making a decision to come home to them, the more influence those benefits will exert. We should try to advance the delivery date of remote benefits so they appear more immediate, and therefore more important, to the adversary. And we should try to postpone, if we cannot eliminate, the drawbacks as they see them of making the decision. The high discount rate in government decision making means that a distant benefit must be large indeed to justify incurring an immediate cost. We should try to reverse this effect. Following the example of commercial salesmen ("Fly now—pay later"), we should try to make the benefits precede the costs: an offer of immediate benefits for future costs. To do so involves some risk that the costs, when they fall due, will somehow be evaded, just as there is a risk that the installment buyer will skip town and fail to make his payments. But the fact that there is a significant default rate on credit sales does not mean that selling on credit is a bad business. In fact it is highly profitable.

In the international situation it is theoretically possible, by advancing the benefits and postponing the costs, to induce a government to make a decision we want and still so structure the situation that they will prefer to accept the costs when they fall due rather than to try to repudiate them and run the risk of incurring still higher costs. While this theoretical model is often hard to apply in particular cases, it does suggest that we should be less insistent than we usually are that the other government perform first. In many cases we will do better in the long run to perform first ourselves, conferring some benefit upon another government, and rely upon implicit moral and political obligations to produce action by the other government. Charles Osgood has developed this approach in his book *An Alternative to War or Surrender* (Urbana: University of Illinois Press, 1962).

GIVE THEM A FADING OPPORTUNITY

Unless there are persuasive reasons for acting today, the tendency is always to wait and see. Postponing a decision enables a government to attempt to get better terms today and still to keep open the option to decide tomorrow. The only cost is one day's delay. In most international conflicts the stakes are high. Benefits to be gained by improving the terms are likely to exceed the cost of waiting one more day. This tendency is likely to recur day after day.

Those who control the agenda exert influence not only by formulating the questions but also by affecting the timing of decisions to be made on them. Part of our offer should make it much more attractive to the adversary to decide today than to delay. We should try to present an adversary government with a fading opportunity. They ought to perceive the decision which we are asking them to make as an opportunity which they will lose if they fail to act soon.

One advantage of offers over threats is that they can more easily be withdrawn before the adversary makes his choice.

Rather than stating a price which is good forever, we should try to arrange offers or opportunities for decision which have an automatic expiration time. There is a great difference between saying "we are always willing to negotiate" and saying "we invite you to send a representative at the ministerial level to meet our representative in Colombo at 11 A.M. local time on Monday the 25th of this month." The first offer is unlikely to be withdrawn. It provides no reason for accepting it on one day rather than the next. To the contrary, there is reason to postpone a decision, hoping that something better may turn up. An offer that

does not expire is like an option that is good indefinitely. It tends not to induce a decision but rather to induce delay while one explores the possibility of better terms. A fading opportunity undercuts the argument within the other government that by failing to decide they can keep their options open.

Though we want to present another government with a reason for deciding now rather than postponing the decision, there are drawbacks to confronting an adversary with a public ultimatum. Either the political cost of giving in to our ultimatum or the precedent which that would establish might be enough to prevent the decision. This problem, however, can be at least partly solved by having the time limits set by a neutral third party, by secret communications, by ambiguity about the deadline, or by constructing the deadline so that it appears to result from facts outside anyone's control.

6

Make the Most of Legitimacy

A LEGITIMATE DEMAND EXERTS INFLUENCE

ONE critical element in any government's decision is their judgment about what they "ought" to do, reflecting their own notions of decency, fair play, morality, order, precedent, international law, and history. We are more likely to be successful in getting an adversary government to make a decision if they believe that it is legitimate—that it has the quality of being the right thing to do. Governments are moved by their own ideas about what is right. We should, therefore, formulate a decision we desire in such a way that it will strike our adversary as a legitimate request.

Bank robbers no doubt realize that what they are doing is wrong, but they do it anyway for personal gain. Governments are different. Government officials, by and large, are people who believe they are acting in the national interest.

They are indoctrinated with advancing the public good, whatever their interpretation of that end may be. They are more likely to ask themselves "What should I do?" than "What can I get away with?" There are, no doubt, exceptions. Some dictators may regard themselves as evil men pursuing personal power for their own pleasure. But a cabinet member in another country is no more likely than a cabinet member in this country to turn to a colleague and say, "It's all a matter of dog eat dog; what do you think we can get away with in our Cuban policy to increase our economic and political gain at their expense?" No. Government officials will argue the Cuban situation in terms of honoring commitments, keeping promises, doing the best thing for the Cuban people, acting in a manner consistent with their own national principles, protecting other nations in Latin America, and so on. Governments tend to think they are pursuing laudable ends by justifiable means.

Margaret Mead has said that the first thing to remember when dealing with other countries is that they think of themselves as being on the side of the right; they see themselves as the good guys. They may be engaged in conduct which we think is evil. But they do not look at it that way. If we characterize a government with whom we are involved in a violent dispute as "aggressors committed to conquest," we should not deceive ourselves into believing that they also regard themselves in that light. The wise course in choosing how to influence another government is to operate on the assumption that they are sincere men who believe, all things considered, that they are pursuing a course of action which is morally right. The fact that they believe this does not, of course, make it true. But if we are trying to influence them, it is their state of mind which is critical.

For one thing, governments need to justify their decisions

within the bureaucracy and to their own citizens. The range of international decisions they can make is circumscribed by their domestic opinion. Lyndon Johnson might well have believed that the cost of total military withdrawal from South Vietnam would be tolerable on the international level. But if he could not convince the American people it was the right course to follow, he would not want to do it. If North Vietnam wants the United States to withdraw, it should be concerned with how withdrawal looks to us—for example, how it is consistent with our notions of self-determination. It will be easier for a government to maintain support and morale at home if they can point out to their own people that making the decision we want them to make is consistent with their own ideas about what is right and what is in their national interests.

Osborn

A major concern of every government is with the precedent set by a given action or decision. If they give in now,
they may open themselves up to giving in again and again.
They will have yielded to pressure and done something
they did not want to do. This fear of setting a harmful
precedent can be overcome by legitimating our demand. If
the decision appears consistent with their principles, no bad
precedent will be set by going along with it. It will be easier
for them to make the decision, and therefore they will be
more likely to make it.

The most important group to whom the demand should
appear legitimate is the group with the decision to make.
Success in getting them to make a decision depends on how
that decision looks in *their* eyes. Attempts to legitimate a
desired decision should start with them in mind. The decision should appear legitimate to the bureaucrats, to the
people who are going to consider it. It should appear so
legitimate that someone will stand up and say, "Here's
something we ought to do." Governments can sometimes
be induced to make decisions they think are improper, but
it is much easier if officials regard a decision they are being
asked to make as morally proper. Officials think of themselves as people who do not make unjustified decisions:
they do not strike back unless justified; they do not retreat
unless justified. So it is their problem of justification we
should deal with first. If we expect them to change their
minds, we must deal with what they think is right and
wrong.

Governments usually formulate demands in just the oppo-
site way: we first try to make the desired decision appear
legitimate in the eyes of our own people. We ask, "What
is the domestic climate? How can we defend to our con-
stituents what we are doing?" We justify our actions in

Vietnam by identifying our adversaries as evil aggressors acting in a grossly illegitimate way. They are murderers and violators of international law. They are behaving outrageously. Such characterization helps rally support for our side both domestically and, perhaps, among third parties. But it makes our adversary even less willing to listen to what we have to say. It makes it less likely that our adversary will make the decision we want. It often makes more likely the failure of our international efforts, with its attendant domestic political costs.

The Soviet Union has emphasized that among the principles on which its foreign policy rests are those of peaceful coexistence, respect for sovereign territory, and noninterference in the internal affairs of other states. The Soviet government is more likely to be influenced if we can convince them that a decision we want is consistent with those principles than they will be if we convince them that it is consistent with the Monroe Doctrine or the principle of free enterprise. The North Vietnamese will be less likely to stay north of the seventeenth parallel, not more, if we argue that to do so is consistent with the containment of Communism. An attempt to point out to an adversary that he ought to make a decision where the "oughtness" is based on *our* ideas of fairness, history, principle, or morality is at best a diversion from the immediate task at hand; at worst it is destructive of the result we want. If changing his mind appears to further his own policy, it will be easier for an adversary to do it. He will only be deterred by arguments that it is consistent with a policy which he thinks of as hostile. If we are attempting to have the Arab states recognize the existence of the state of Israel and to get Israel to withdraw from territory occupied by force of arms, a speech in the United Nations devoted to justifying for our own home audience a general posture toward the Middle East situation is at best a waste of time.

If we begin by making our objective legitimate to the home audience, we may also tie our hands. The British justified their sanctions against Rhodesia by labeling Ian Smith a traitor. They subsequently found themselves under considerable criticism for agreeing to negotiate with traitors. We are likely to limit our capability to make concessions, to negotiate, or to change our position in any substantial way without appearing to be selling out our principles. We will lose the flexibility that comes from formulating an objective which is consistent with two points of view.

It is not hard to understand why the more consistent a request can be made with another government's notions of right and wrong, with their principles and values, the more reason they will have to grant it. In 1966 an American student touring Russia was apprehended and convicted for stealing an iron statue of a bear. The American lawyers who helped appeal the case did not attempt to argue that the Russian court should have sympathy for this young American, or that in his trial he had been denied due process. Instead they turned to the grounds for punishment authorized in the Soviet statute. The only relevant one was "rehabilitation to conform to Soviet standards of morality." They pointed out that for this particular crime the reasons for punishment did not apply, since the best way to prevent further violations of Soviet morality would be to expel the youth. They did not argue that the Russian rules were bad ones. They said, "But your rules say you should turn this man loose and send him out of the country." The argument was directed at making the request legitimate in the eyes of the Soviet judge according to his own principles. For the first time in a case like this, the appeal was successful.

It is desirable that our demands should appear legitimate to third parties as well. They can exert independent influence, and even if they take no action, their views will make a difference. An adversary government will incur an increased political cost by refusing to go along with a decision which third parties regard as fair. And we reduce the political cost to ourselves of pressing the demand. Further, the fact that the demand seems fair to third parties will itself make it seem more legitimate to the adversary. But legitimating the demand in the eyes of the adversary is still more important than legitimating it in the eyes of others. To demonstrate that a demand is legitimate because it is consistent with precedent, or because it affects both sides equally, lets an adversary make the decision without adverse effects on third parties or on our own public opinion. If our adversary thinks the demand is legitimate, so will third parties.

LEGITIMACY IS BETTER FOR PEACE

We should also formulate legitimate demands because it will be better for the international system in the long run. Our foreign policy has two underlying objectives. We want to win. And we want to maintain international law and order; we want disputes settled by a fair and orderly procedure. These objectives are somewhat inconsistent. We would like to win each dispute, but we do not want a system in which we win every dispute. We could not expect other countries to lie down peacefully and tolerate such a world. The more legitimate our demands are, the better we will be able to achieve both objectives. As we consider what it is we ought to adopt as our objective in Cyprus, Thailand, or Cuba, we will want to appreciate the degree to which adopting one goal rather than another will better serve our continuing interest in a peaceful world. The clearer it is both to us and to the rest of the world that the goal we are seeking is legitimate and that we are seeking it by legitimate means, the less disruptive our actions will be to international order. We should seek to influence the style in which other nations pursue their policy by the style in which we conduct ours. And the legitimacy of our objectives is affected more by their selection and formulation than by the rhetoric we advance in their behalf.

SOME WAYS TO FORMULATE LEGITIMATE DEMANDS

One way to legitimate our demands is to have our objective—the decision we want another government to make—closely related to that government's past actions. Most international disputes are concerned with events which have already occurred. One side charges the other with having broken an agreement, violated rights, or committed an outrage of one kind or another. But what has happened is water over the dam. The past has significance only as it affects the future. We usually overlook the fact that the sole reason for a government's communicating a judgment about the past is to affect the future—in our case to influence what another government will do. We may be interested in knowing privately the facts regarding the justification which Israel had for launching its military offensive in June of 1967 so that we will be better able to predict what the Israeli (and Arab) leaders are likely to do in other circumstances. Such knowledge may also help us to identify some realistic and attainable objectives. But the primary reason for our making public statements about Israel's conduct and for characterizing it in one way or another should be for the purpose of legitimation. Our rhetoric may help make more legitimate (in the eyes of those we are trying to influence, in our own eyes, or in the eyes of bystanders) what we are asking for, what we are offering, or what we are threatening. For example: "Israel should withdraw from territory it has occupied in 1967 because . . ." "In view of what happened last month it would be proper to sell arms to the government of Jordan if they should first . . ." "In view of the uses to which such funds have been put in the past, the Treasury Department is re-examining the deductibility as contributions to a domestic charity of funds destined for Israel."

One way to use the past for legitimation is to formulate decisions in such a way that they appear similar to, or at least consistent with, previous decisions made by the adversary or other governments under similar circumstances. Governments find it easier to do things which have been done before. Not all precedents are good; the adversary government may not even like the precedent we are invoking. But they will usually feel that the risk of serious criticism of action for which there is a precedent is less than the risk involved in doing something which has never been done before. Suppose our government discovers that a foreign diplomat is engaging in espionage. To ask that he apologize and give a formal undertaking not to do it again might be an extremely reasonable request—but without precedent. Therefore his government would probably find it difficult to decide that he should give such an undertaking. On the other hand, a request that his government withdraw him would almost certainly be granted. The latter would be effective not because we were asking for less, but because there are many precedents for the recall of a diplomat upon the request of another government.

If, in order to increase the chances of an Israeli withdrawal from occupied territory after the 1967 war, we were pressing Jordan to recognize the state of Israel, we might well have concluded that this demand was not within the realm of the possible. It was politically difficult for Jordan to make such a statement, and under the circumstances Jordan would not consider such a demand legitimate. We might have changed the words we were asking for, and by finding words for which there was some precedent give Jordan a proposition which would appear to them more legitimate. We might, for example, have asked King Hussein to make a speech saying that Jordan "reaffirms all her obligations under the United Nations Charter to all members of the United Nations," thus affording tacit recognition of Israel. In making such a demand we would *not* have pointed out to Jordan the unreasonableness of past statements threatening to use force against Israel and tried to persuade them to reverse themselves. We would have pointed out that if they desired Israeli withdrawal, it would be necessary to undercut the legitimacy of the Israeli position. We could have said, "We've gone through your official statements. In 1951 you said such and such. In 1959 you said thus and so." We could pick out statements in which Jordan came close to recognizing Israel. Then we would say, "All we're doing is asking you to rephrase slightly these past policy statements." The Jordanians would have had the opportunity, at least, to say, "Well, that's not so bad. If we've done this before we can defend going a little further. We won't even be abandoning the Arab line too much, since we made all those statements in the past." Our ability to show that under comparable circumstances comparable action has been taken will make it easier for an adversary government to satisfy themselves and others that what we are asking them to do is the right thing to do.

There are other ways in which the past can be used to lend legitimacy to our present demands. The fact that an adversary has in the past promised to do something makes it more legitimate to ask for it now. Or if an adversary has done something in the past, we may be able to relate our demands to that action on a tit-for-tat basis. A demand will also be more legitimate if it apparently seeks to restore the *status quo ante*. In the Cuban missile crisis, President Kennedy's demand that the missiles be removed from Cuba looked legitimate because Russia's action was identified as a radical change from the pre-existing balance of force in the hemisphere. Israel is a threat to the Arab countries because it disrupts a status; it represents an alarming rate of change. But the fact that Israel has been in existence for twenty years gives it far more legitimacy to the Arabs than it had the day it was established.

Another way to legitimate our demands is to use the form and language of reciprocity. A demand will be more legitimate if it appears to affect both sides in the same way. A Ho Chi Minh suggestion that all troops except those native to South Vietnam be removed appeared more legitimate than President Johnson's suggestion that the United States stop its troop increases and that North Vietnam stop troop increases, troop replacements, and the sending in of supplies.

Changing the demand to ask for agreement on a procedural rather than a substantive step can make the demand more legitimate if the procedure has a built-in "fairness" to both sides. In Vietnam our objective was sometimes identified as a non-Communist government for South Vietnam and sometimes as a government freely chosen by the people of South Vietnam. The second formulation is obviously more legitimate to adversaries of the United States.

We can legitimate our demands by justifying them in terms of international law. The fact that there is often disagreement about points of international law has obscured the extent to which international law determines what governments want and what they are willing to do. International politics rests upon foundations which are basically legal ones. Governments are legal institutions. They exercise authority over countries which are defined by legal boundaries. A country's government and its public become upset or not depending upon their view of their legal rights. We defend what we think we are entitled to defend. The existence of legal boundaries is crucial in organizing political forces. Suppose a volcano erupted and created a new island off the Aleutians. If the Russians began landing troops there, the central question in everyone's mind would be, "Is that island theirs or ours?" If it were theirs, we would expect them to put troops there. If it were ours, their action would be intolerable. We would get upset. We would have to defend our national boundaries from aggression. Whether such an island is ours or theirs is a legal question influenced by legal arguments based on maps, treaty clauses, prior discovery, occupation, and so forth. If we heard that Chinese troops had marched to within 300 miles of New Delhi, our political reaction would depend less on the physical fact than on a question of law. The first thing we would want to know is where the Indian-Chinese boundary was located.

Governments are, of course, influenced by economic and military considerations. They are also influenced by a good legal case. At a time when the United States government had a general trade embargo against Cuba, they returned boats and aircraft that were stolen from the Cuban government by refugees fleeing to the United States. We were persuaded to accede to the request of the Cuban government at this time because of the strength of their legal case. To be sure, political consequences at home and abroad were taken into account, but to a large extent these political consequences themselves depended on the legal question. The more demonstrable it was that a boat legally belonged to the Cuban government, the more it made political sense to send it back to them. This being true, a government improves their chances of success by asking for things to which they are legally entitled. They also improve their chance of success by doing what they can to demonstrate to their adversary's satisfaction that they are legally entitled to what they are asking for.

There is an unfortunate tendency to conclude either that international law is all-important or that it is unimportant. Neither is true. Our almost instinctive views about our rights and obligations enormously affect our basic perception of what we want and what we are trying to accomplish. Were we attacked by Mexico, we would not ask whether a few acres in Texas were really worth defending. The rightness and wrongness—the legal case—comes in immediately. Similarly, no one in our government is comparing the benefits in land, power, and prestige which might be gained through conquering Mexico against the costs which would be involved. Such a conquest would be wrong. Today it would take unusual circumstances to raise the question of our conquering territory to which we had no legal right. An unconscious perception of the national interest is formed by existing legal arrangements. By consciously forming our objectives where our legal case is strong, and will appear strong to those we are trying to influence, we make it easier to succeed. By demonstrating to an adversary government the strength of our legal claim, we make it far easier for them to agree to it.

Another way of legitimating a request is to have it reflect the view of an impartial third party. This is most effective when the request comes initially from a third party who is obviously independent. If the first call for negotiations in Vietnam had come from the Soviet Union or the Organization of African Unity rather than from the government of the United States, North Vietnam might have found the request easier to accept. A demand for a cease-fire which comes from the Secretary-General or the Security Council of the United Nations is usually more acceptable than one which comes from an adversary. The fact that the call for a cease-fire in the Middle East in June, 1967, came from the United Nations probably made it more effective than it would have been had it come from Russia or the United States, or even from both of those countries together.

During the Cuban missile crisis of October, 1962, the United States government was in urgent need of support to legitimate their request that the Soviet missiles be withdrawn. The unanimous vote of the Organization of American States in support of the quarantine against Soviet missiles did much to make President Kennedy's demand legitimate. To some extent this must have made it easier for the Soviet Union to withdraw the missiles than would have been the case had the vote gone the other way or even had a few of the Latin American governments disagreed and said that the missiles should stay. The endorsement of the United States demand by some Latin American countries which have had the reputation for routinely kowtowing to the United States no doubt had less effect than the endorsement by such countries as Mexico and Brazil, which had established reputations for independence. The perceived legitimacy of the OAS demand was one distinct element in a successful attempt at influence, an attempt which included a narrow, yesable demand, a risk of serious consequences if the desired decision was not made, an attractive prospect (a pledge not to invade Cuba) if the decision was made, and face-saving. The decision we were asking the Soviet Union to make was legitimated in terms of the *status quo ante*, the views of impartial third parties and international organizations, past promises (it is difficult to believe that Soviet officials regarded the missiles as "defensive"), and history. This legitimation undoubtedly played a role in getting the Soviet Union to change their mind.

To exert influence by demonstrating the fairness of our requests we need a large reservoir of truly independent countries. I think we have underestimated the value to us of neutral countries. A General Assembly which in the early days often behaved as if it were a rubber stamp for the United States could do less for us than can the present Assembly which has shown its independence. To have our objective endorsed by "lackeys and puppets" will not legitimate it at all in the eyes of a hostile government. For this reason it may be that the United States has been shortsighted in so often making an effort to convert fair-minded governments into allies who can be routinely counted upon to support us on almost any question, regardless of the merits. We value too highly small victories which are achieved through arm-twisting in the General Assembly. Both we and the United Nations would often gain more through the demonstrated independence of other governments. As a government under law we can take losses. A reputation for bias in our favor makes it impossible for another government to exert much influence in our favor. One would rather have a fair-minded friend in the jury box than at the counsel table.

A good way to legitimate an objective is to defer in advance to the views or decision of a third party. A government may call on an adversary to submit the dispute to arbitration or to the views of some other impartial body. This method is useful not only for legitimating requests but also for legitimating action taken in furtherance of an objective. When the United Arab Republic refused to comply with a Security Council decision on Suez it greatly strengthened its case by saying that its action was subject to review by the International Court of Justice: If any signatory of the Constantinople Convention of 1888 wanted to contend that the U.A.R. should take Israel-bound cargo, the U.A.R. agreed to accept the jurisdiction of the International Court and be bound by its decision. This was a useful thing to do. The Egyptians were saying, "We think we are right. There is the Court. If you think we are wrong, take it to the Court."

When the United States gave military aid to Greece and Turkey in 1947, the Congress, at the instigation of Senator Arthur Vandenberg, provided that if at any time the Security Council should ask us to get out, all military personnel would be withdrawn and that for that purpose the United States renounced its right of veto in the Security Council. Had a Council resolution actually been passed, we might have chosen to ignore it. But that clause greatly increased the legitimacy of our intervention. American military intervention in the Dominican Republic in 1965 could have been accomplished with far less political cost had we legitimated our action there by such an arrangement. We could have stated that we were going in as neutrals and not on one

side or the other of the conflict; that our military forces
were there only pending maintenance of law and order by
the Organization of American States; and that as soon as
the OAS or the United Nations felt that they had the capability to keep the peace and asked us to leave, we would
do so. The OAS would have been extremely unlikely to ask
us, by the necessary two-thirds-majority vote, to leave. Even
if they had, we might have taken some time to withdraw.
Our statement that we would get out under such circumstances would have made our intervention more tolerable
for others and less damaging for us.

THE THREAT AND THE OFFER SHOULD BE LEGITIMATE

Not only is it important to so formulate a desired decision
that an adversary feels he ought to make it. It is also important to legitimate the consequences which will flow from
that decision. The offer and the threat should seem legitimate to the other government by their own standards. An
offer will exert more influence if it is a set of consequences
which appear to flow naturally and inevitably from the
decision we would like the adversary to make. An offer will
not exert favorable influence—perhaps the reverse—if it
appears to be a bribe. A bribe, to be successful, should not
look like a bribe. Instead it should appear to the adversary
government to be something to which they would be properly entitled if they made the decision—a decision which is
proper for other reasons.

One other way to legitimate our offers is to use the vocabulary and the rhetoric—the terms of reference—of the adversary. We must consider what we can say about an offer
which will make it more legitimate. United States aid pro-

grams are to some extent more effective because they have become recognized not as charity but as a moral obligation of the United States. Underdeveloped countries can now identify aid as the fulfillment of our obligation to help and support them, and can more easily accept aid without incurring any political cost. But we should consider how the offer of a particular aid program looks to the country to which we are offering it. In April, 1965, we offered to give $1 billion in economic assistance to both Vietnams if peace could be restored. As I noted in Chapter 5, to leaders who had fought for years for national independence and against foreign influence, the prospect of indefinite American financial involvement in Southeast Asian development may have looked more like a cost than a benefit. Even if those the offer was designed to influence placed a high value on the monetary assistance, and even if they thought the offer was highly credible, it probably looked to them like a bribe. A neocolonialist white power says, "Sell out your war of liberation and we will pay you off in dollars." They would not want to admit to themselves or to others that the political goals for which they were striving could be abandoned in exchange for a sum of money. In fact, the political cost to a government of accepting something that looks like a bribe may exceed any substantive benefit that would result. The political sensitivity of some public officials is like that of a maiden: to try to improve a proposition with a cash offer may lead to frustration rather than to success. We could have made that offer more legitimate if, as suggested, it had been put in different terms. The United States could still have regarded it as a gift, but it could have been so offered that North Vietnam would be free to regard it as war reparations. Such an arrangement would have been more legitimate in the eyes of North Vietnam. It would have been far more attractive. It would have exerted more influence.

Another way to legitimate an offer is to coordinate the consequences of the decision with the decision itself. It is of doubtful legitimacy to say to another government, "We will not give you any fertilizer unless you improve your tax program." However it would be legitimate to offer to send them fertilizer if they would use it efficiently or to offer technical assistance on a new tax system if they would commit themselves to adopt one. An offer to pay a certain sum of money to a country if they would paint their government buildings green looks like internal interference of the most outrageous sort. But to say, "We will give you some green paint free if you would like to paint your government buildings with it," is not interference but generosity.

A threat which seems legitimate to our adversaries will also exert more influence than one which appears to be unjustified blackmail. Governments have a natural reluctance to yield to a threat of force. Again, they are more likely to change their mind if the consequences which will result from their not making the decision we want them to make appear to flow naturally and inevitably from that decision. Any action we are talking about taking should appear to be something we ought to do, will have to do, would naturally do, or at least would be entitled to do. Again, it is the state of mind of the adversary which is important: we should attempt to legitimate the threat in *their* eyes. If the government we are trying to influence believes that the threat is a fair one, they will find it easier to yield to it.

No matter how laudable the objective in the mind of the government making a threat, if the situation looks like blackmail the government being asked to yield will see no end to the subsequent demands that might be made and supported by the same threat. Yielding to an illegitimate threat sets a bad precedent that may look to a government like a high cost. It should appear to them not that they are "giving in" but rather that they are acting in their own self-interest to avoid the natural costs of a certain course of action. If so, the precedent which will be set will be much less damaging to them.

Furthermore, a legitimate threat is a more credible threat. Since implementing the threat will be less politically costly to us, they know that we will be more likely to do it. A legitimate threat is safer because there is less risk of their making a counterthreat—less risk of retaliation. It will be easier to justify to our own people both making and implementing a threat if it is legitimate.

The task of making a threat legitimate may involve legitimating what is said at the time the threat is communicated, legitimating what is done to make the threat credible, and legitimating the action we take in implementing the threat. The best way to make a threat legitimate is to relate it closely in time, place, and subject matter to the demand—to the precise decision we are asking another government to make. Unpleasant consequences which are logically related to a decision will usually appear fairer, less provocative, and more acceptable. A related threat will not only have a greater chance of success, but will also tend to limit the conflict to the subject matter of the threat and the decision. A related threat tends to exert more influence not only because it is legitimate but also because it is closely aimed at those who have a decision to make. I have said that the most effective threat may be a threat to impose the desired result by self-help if an adversary refuses to bring it about by making the decision. "If your ambassador does not remove his car from in front of the fire hydrant, we will tow it away." "If you do not decide to stop your troops at the border, we will stop them there." If the demand is legitimate, a related self-help type of threat is highly legitimate. And there is less risk of increasing the conflict.

Where a threat is not limited to bringing about the desired result, it is still more legitimate if it is related to the subject matter of the demand. A threat to let the air out of the tires of an illegally parked car is more legitimate than a threat to inflict unrelated harm such as breaking a window in the house of the owner. An adversary finds it difficult to yield to an unrelated threat, because it tends to look like unprincipled blackmail. Economic sanctions, for example, usually suffer from the illegitimacy which comes from being unrelated. They constitute action taken against a country as a whole because its government failed to make a political decision unrelated to the imposition of sanctions. Indiscriminate bombing tends to be illegitimate because the injury imposed cannot be justified except on the broad ground that the end justifies the means, a proposition which is in itself hard to justify. It is not surprising that, within the United States, the most effective threats in support of civil rights have been those of action which was highly legitimate and closely related to the immediate objective. A lunchroom sit-in is more legitimate than a march or a demonstration in the streets, and is likely to be more effective. The element of inflicting pain for the sake of inflicting pain is absent. The threat is: "I intend to sit here until I am served because I have a right to sit here and I have a right to be served." In the Montgomery bus boycott, Negroes said that unless they could sit in unsegregated seats on public busses, they would not ride in them. Effort spent in support of such related threats tends to be more effective than comparable

effort in support of unrelated threats. In international politics, demonstrations in front of embassies and the burning
of libraries are ineffective not only because they are irrelevant to the action requested but also because, being irrelevant, they are illegitimate.

In Vietnam the United States felt rightly it should justify
its conduct in bombing North Vietnam in terms of the im-
mediacy of the relationship between the bombing and the
infiltration which it was designed to stop. The threat to
bomb urban areas was made credible by bombing some.
This threat to bomb targets unrelated to infiltration was a
threat of greater pain, yet it appeared to all concerned so
illegitimate that it lost effectiveness on that account. On
March 31, 1968, bombing north of latitude 19° or 20° was
stopped. It had long been suggested to the government
that a continuing threat to bomb south of a line drawn
across North Vietnam, in order to identify the bombing as
a self-help measure to stop infiltration near the border of
North and South, would have been a much more legitimate
and perhaps a much more effective threat.

7

Law and Legal Institutions May Help

IT IS worth while considering explicitly how international law and institutions fit into the process of causing another government to change their mind. Here the going gets rough, because there is such widespread misunderstanding of how law works—misunderstanding both among advocates of international law and among its detractors. Although I cannot expect in a few words to convert anyone from a deeply held belief, I can at least articulate my own views. I will do so by setting up and dealing with three straw men—men who may, in fact, not be made exclusively of straw. I will then illustrate in terms of the Cuban missile case the kind of diverse roles which law and legal institutions can be expected to play in exerting influence upon another government.

The following three statements reflect the views of a substantial number of people:

1. "Law works because it is a command backed up by force."
2. "It takes force to influence another government."
3. "Law operates as a restraint, and it cannot restrain a government from doing what they want."

Each of these statements is essentially false. In each case there is an element of truth underlying the statement, but the generalization is wrong. It would be a serious mistake to rely on any one of these propositions in deciding what to do. Let us look at them one at a time.

Fallacy No. 1: "Law works because it is a command backed up by force."

There is a tendency to make a distinction between international law and "real" law, which is backed up by force. The argument then goes that since international law is not backed up by force, the kind of law which works domestically cannot be expected to work internationally. But the premise is wrong. For those in whose conduct we are interested—national governments—domestic law is backed up by less force than is international law. The process by which national governments are controlled by domestic law is more than an analogy; it demonstrates the susceptibilities of the very governments we are interested in.

The command theory of law, which was used to distinguish the law that *is* from the law that *ought to be*, was developed out of an examination of the typical private action for a tort or on a contract. If a court declared that a defendant must pay a plaintiff a stated amount, the sheriff and the marshal stood ready to enforce the judgment with the full power of the state.

That was the situation envisioned by the legal philosopher

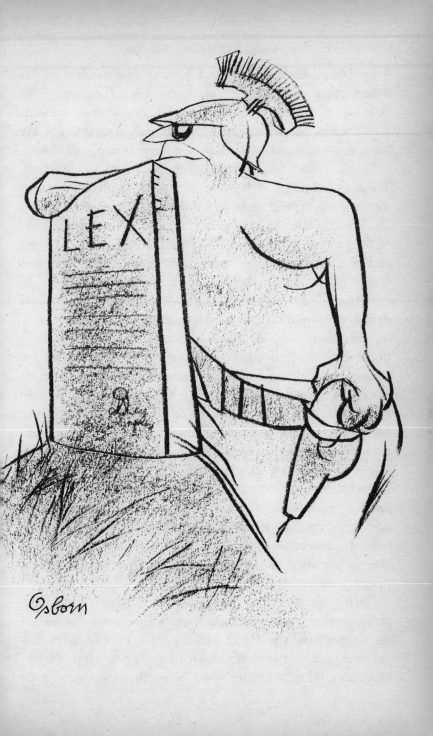

John Austin when he spoke of laws as commands. But his definition of law did not apply to rules restraining the behavior of a state. The "power of the government," he said, "is incapable of *legal* limitation." It followed that, in his view, a government had neither legal rights nor legal duties.

Such a definition of law has no relevance to our problem. We are concerned exclusively with the conduct of governments. In a typical year, more than half the cases before the United States Supreme Court involve the rights or duties of the federal government, all of which are considered legal and are dealt with by legal institutions. The command theory of law—the notion that domestic law works because it is backed up by superior force—is plainly wrong when dealing with public law. Governments regularly comply with adverse court decisions. This is true not only for constitutional law, administrative law, and tax law, but even for criminal law. When a man charged with crime is acquitted, and the court orders the government to release him, the government does so, and they do so not because they are compelled to do so by a threat of force superior to that of the government. When a judgment is entered against the United States in the Court of Claims, no superior sovereign compels Congress to vote the appropriation. Legal limitations upon a government, whether they be those of constitutional law or international law, succeed or fail for reasons other than the existence of superior military force. By and large law with respect to governments works because it affects political consequences, not military ones.

During the course of the Korean War, the steel industry of the United States was threatened with a strike. Considering the pros and cons as they then looked, President Truman decided to seize the steel industry in order to keep it operating and did so. The steel companies disputed the government's right to seize the industry and took the matter to court. After a few weeks of litigation the Supreme Court ordered the Secretary of Commerce, who had taken charge of the steel mills at the President's request, to return them to their private owners.

The Supreme Court had no regiments at its command. It had no greater force vis-à-vis the government than does the International Court of Justice sitting at The Hague. Yet the steel mills were returned. There can be little doubt that in a showdown between "the government" and the Supreme Court, the government would have won. If the President had wanted to continue to hold the steel mills, the army would have obeyed him.

The government had a choice when taking over the steel mills. They decided that the national interest made the action desirable. The legal process worked because it changed the question with which the government were confronted—in a number of respects.

Before the Court spoke, the demand upon the government was both vague and general. If articulated by the management of the steel companies, it would have been that the government must never seize private property without specific legal authority. So far as the demand came from the Constitution, it was a general rule, coming from no one in particular and going to no one in particular. So far as the demand came from the steel companies, it came from biased persons with a personal interest in the outcome. The consequences to the government of yielding to the demand may have looked serious. To allow steel production to stop because of a strike while American soldiers were dying in Korea would have produced a hostile political reaction within the United States. It also might have affected the conduct of the war. To accept the proposition that in time of emergency the government could do nothing to keep the most important industry operating would establish a disastrous precedent. The consequences of seizing the steel industry were more attractive. At the worst, somebody might take the case to court, and the government could face that problem when and if it arose.

The decision of the Court changed the demand. It now came from a respected and disinterested body and was directed to a named individual, the Secretary of Commerce. The decision was not in the form of a general restriction against interfering with private property, but a narrow and explicit demand that he refrain from asserting further authority over the steel companies' property. The fact and form of the demand also changed the consequences of the government's decision. So far as internal politics was concerned, it now made more sense to go along with the Supreme Court than to defy it. Further, the precedent which would be established by going along with the Court's decision became a favorable one from the point of view of the government rather than an unfavorable one. On the other hand, to defy the Court's decision would establish a disastrous precedent which others might follow. Finally, the decision of the Court was narrowly directed at the particular way in which the government had acted. To accept the decision was merely to take one step back. The same end could be pursued by the government by other means.

Law enforcement against a government involves not a command backed up by force. Rather it involves so changing the choice with which the government is confronted that their long-range interest in orderly settlement of disputes outweighs their short-run interest in winning this particular dispute.

This is also, I believe, a more useful way of understanding

the process than to talk of shared values and a sense of community. Shared values and a sense of community will help the legal process operate and will set limits on what it can do, but they fail to shed light on the process itself. Shared values and a sense of community, by themselves, are not enough to cause a government to respect the law. The routine violation of law by federal officers in the cases of wire tapping and unlawful searches and seizures amply demonstrates that the United States government cannot be counted on to comply with the law whenever they know what it is. I am convinced that the same officers who would violate a general restriction would comply with a narrow and explicit court injunction ordering them by name not to tap a particular telephone. Such a demand would shift the political situation. A court decision can be looked at as influencing a government to change their mind not so much by adding new weight to one side of a question as by shifting the fulcrum so that political forces which were previously on one side of the balance now find themselves on the other.

Domestic courts may thus be taken as a model not only for how international courts may be expected to exert influence on governments but for other international institutions as well. Although we may not expect the statement of an international body to carry the same political impact upon a government as does the legally binding decision of their own court, its impact will be greater the more its statement resembles that of a domestic court. The steel companies influenced the United States government not by threatening to hurt the government by retaliatory action but by going through third-party procedures which changed the question. The steel companies took the risk that the decision would not be to their liking. In exchange, they gained the effective political support which followed a decision in their favor.

Fallacy No. 2: "It takes force to influence another government."

Although we can accept the idea that our own government is influenced by considerations other than force in "domestic" questions, we tend to believe that on international questions it takes force to exert influence on other governments. But every decision of a government is a domestic one in the sense that it is made by a domestic government. Whatever the nominal subject, governmental officers are affected by the anticipated consequences of a decision both within and without the territorial limits of the country. In terms of the character of the considerations which affect a decision there is no sharp line between domestic decisions and international decisions. And underlying this entire book is the idea that no one ingredient of the influence process is either all-important or unimportant. Force is relevant but not all-important. In some cases it will be necessary, in others insufficient. A government will take into account the whole picture as they see it. In one situation the greatest hope of exerting influence may lie in changing one element; in another situation it will lie in changing another element, or in changing several at the same time.

To confirm the limited role which force plays—and to suggest opportunities for law and legal institutions—let me pull together from previous chapters some conclusions about other things that do exert influence upon another government:

Make the desired decision explicit. The more unambiguous the request the easier it is for a government to deal with.

Make the request one for inaction rather than action. If the decision desired is not only reformulated but is reformulated in such a way that, rather than requiring a new decision, the request will be met if the other government fails to make a decision to act contrary to the request, the chance of success is further increased.

Have the request come from a neutral party. If the revised request comes from an impartial source, there is a greater likelihood that the government will make the desired decision. The political cost of going along with a neutral request is far less than that of "giving in" to an adversary. In fact, under these circumstances, to decide as desired tends to establish a helpful procedural precedent, rather than a harmful one.

Have the request formed in terms of principles accepted by the other government. If the proposed decision is formulated as one which is required by standards, policies, or rules accepted by the government we are trying to influence, it will be more readily acceptable to that government's officers. They may even regard it as their duty to go along with it.

Have the request narrowly limited to the next step. The immediate cost of yielding to a request will be less if less is asked.

Change the decision desired. To present a government with a different decision than the one they had previously declined to make both provides an occasion for decision and permits a decision we would like without requiring a reversal of position.

Such actions tend to increase the chance of success. They do so by altering the three basic elements of demand, offer, and threat. They reform the decision we want into one that is institutionally easier for a government to make; they tend to reduce the political cost of acting in accordance with our wishes and to increase the political cost of not doing so.

The above summary of important ways to exert influence on governments turns out to be also a summary of important ways in which international institutions can deal with an international dispute. These elements of the process of exerting influence are those which international institutions are in general equipped to perform. Other elements of the process of exerting influence upon a government, in particular increasing a risk of military action, tend to be those at which international institutions are not very good. Much of the current lack of regard for the capabilities of international organizations stems from misperceiving the task to be done. Only if the crucial task in exerting influence upon a government were to increase the military threat would it be correct to minimize the role which international organizations might be expected to play.

When a dispute is referred to an international institution, whether it be the General Assembly, the Security Council, the International Court of Justice, or an *ad hoc* tribunal, commission, or committee of any kind, the foundation has been laid for changing the question facing each government. Each government will be more influenced by what the international institution asks than by what an adversary asks. This does not, of course, mean that governments will always do what they are asked to do by an international institution or that they will never do what they are asked by another government.

A decision or recommendation of an international institution typically asks of a government something less than what was asked of them by their adversary. A neutral institution is freed from the temptation to include something extra in its demand to give it negotiating room. On the contrary, no further bargaining is usually anticipated, and the institution will recognize that the less it asks, the greater the chance of compliance with its request.

Even where it asks no less, the institution can be extremely explicit about what it is asking for. The demand also comes from a neutral. Each of these facts tends to make it politically easier for a government to yield to the demand.

It has long been pointed out that if governments have agreed to international arbitration, they usually abide by the result. This fact is sometimes cited in support of the proposition that all governments ought to agree to compulsory arbitration or adjudication. Others cite it to support the proposition that arbitration only works where governments are prepared to abide by the result. From our point of view the interesting fact is that governments find it much easier to go along with a request if it is made by an impartial body of recognized authority than if a comparable request is made by an adversary. If prior to an arbitrator's decision a government's weighing of the pros and cons results in a political decision not to do what it is being asked to do, and after the arbitrator's decision the government's weighing of the pros and cons comes out differently, this may be because they are being asked to do something different. Whether or not that is true, the consequences of the choice have been changed.

From the point of view of a lawyer there is a black-and-white difference between international decisions which are legally binding upon a government and those that are not. From the point of view of the student of government behavior the matter is one of degree. One of the features of a decision which gives it political power is the quality of being regarded by some as legally binding. Other features are also important, and in terms of political consequences even the legal question tends to be one of degree.

Fallacy No. 3: "Law operates as a restraint, and it cannot restrain a government from doing what they want."

There are two parts to this statement. That law and legal institutions do exert influence suggests what is wrong with the second part of the statement. In one sense law cannot restrain a government from doing what they want, but law affects what they want. In the absence of a legal rule to the contrary, the United States government might well conclude that they wanted to take over the oil fields of Kuwait. The existence of a rule of international law which makes it improper for the United States to seize the oil fields of Kuwait results in the United States government's not wanting to seize the fields. Law, by affecting what governments want, does restrain them from doing things which they would otherwise want to do.

The first part of the statement is also misleading. Law, to be sure, does operate as a restraint, but it does far more than that. To think of law only as a restraint on behavior is to underestimate its potential. Law and legal institutions play many roles. Unfortunately, from the point of view of exposition by an international lawyer, law and legal institutions become relevant in a number of quite disconnected ways at different points in the international political process. And at each one of these points nonlegal considerations may be more important than legal ones. There may be good reason to rely not on the law or on the courts but on other norms and other institutions. We may choose to rely not on a legal contract but on a gentleman's agreement. A man's reputation may provide us with more security than could any remedy at law. A recommendation from the governing board of a stock exchange may have more impact than a court decision.

Lawyers are rightly skeptical about a book such as "Law of the Theater" which tries to pull together the diverse roles which law and legal institutions play in a particular business. Such a book will cover bits and pieces of law dealing with copyright, options, the leasing of theaters, the making and breaking of contracts, local regulation and censorship, liability for negligence, the right of privacy, and perhaps something on slander and libel. If a man wishes to put on a theatrical performance which is artistically and financially successful, the law and its institutions may help him to do so, but they are unlikely to be the most important consideration. What theater he rents is likely to be more important than the terms of the lease, what actors he hires more important than the terms of their contracts, and what the critics say about the play more important than what the lawyers say about it. Yet to ignore the law would be risky. It provides both opportunities for making success easier and defenses against problems which might otherwise lead to failure.

The role of law and institutions in the pursuit by a government of an international objective is not unlike their role in the pursuit by a businessman or theatrical producer of some objective of his. Law is not just a restraint. To ask only the question "will our conduct be legal" is to omit consideration of most of the ways in which law can serve the enterprise. In influencing another government as in

putting on a play, law is not the most important consideration, but a knowledgeable use of the opportunities which
law and legal institutions offer can make success more likely.

The variety of ways in which international law and legal
institutions do and do not affect government decisions can
be illustrated by looking at the predominantly nonlegal
decisions of the United States government in October, 1962,
on what to do about the Soviet introduction of intermediate-
and long-range missiles into Cuba. The following brief
analysis is based on the accounts of the missile crisis by
Elie Abel and Theodore Sorensen.

The motive for United States action was not primarily to
maintain or improve the international system, but rather
to pursue political and military objectives within the system.
We should expect law to play modest roles in decisions
which were primarily concerned with things other than
the law.

International law implicitly affected what the United
States wanted. The action which caused the United States
government to have a problem on its hands was the secret
placing in Cuba of intermediate- and long-range missiles
and bomber aircraft by the Soviet Union after they had
previously assured the United States that they were not
doing so and were not going to do so. Officials of the United
States knew that they did not like what had happened and
what was going on. In the discussions, they apparently did
not consider separately alternative objectives that the
United States might pursue, but only alternative courses
of action the United States might follow. In a general way
the objective was clear. The United States wanted the missiles not to become operable with nuclear warheads and
wanted to be confident that this was the case. Alternative
formulations of the objective might have been to have the

missiles come into United States possession or to be destroyed or damaged or removed from Cuba.

International law had little to do with this objective. The United States wanted the missiles to become inoperable independent of its legal rights. But international law did play a crucial role in creating the problem. What made the United States response so difficult was the fact that the Soviet Union had apparently acted within its legal rights under international law. If the Soviet Union had installed the missiles on an island in the Caribbean belonging to the United States, or on an unoccupied corner of Alaska—in clear violation of international law—the United States would have been presented with a problem that looked totally different. The fact that the provocative act of the Soviet Union was not illegal and the fact that the objective desired by the United States was not one to which it was automatically entitled as a matter of international law were both central to the crisis.

International law affected what the United States decided to try for. It affected, implicitly if not explicitly, the selection of the three narrow objectives: having the weapons now in Cuba removed, having no further offensive weapons sent to Cuba, and having some form of international verification. No doubt the United States military authorities would have liked to acquire the Soviet missiles, both those in Cuba and those heading toward Cuba, and studied them. But the Soviet Union still had legal ownership of the missiles. If the Soviet Union were willing to withdraw the missiles from Cuba, the United States had no legal right to seize those missiles, or even to destroy them. There was no legal case for saying that missiles on board a ship bound for Cuba had thereby become contraband and forfeited to the United States government.

International law provided a set of tools. Influence requires communication. One of the functions of law is to serve as a language. International law helps one government communicate to another about the choice with which they are confronted and about the consequences of making or not making the desired decision. If a government has embarked upon a course of action, as the Soviet government had in Cuba, the issue must be reopened. Law and legal institutions can help present a government with a new occasion for decision. They can also clarify and alter both the decision that is required and the consequences of making and of not making that decision.

Legal documents tend to be far more precise than most political statements. A simple reference to an established rule of law can convey a great deal of meaning because of what is incorporated.

The resolution adopted by the Organization of American States, the draft resolution submitted to the United Nations, and the proclamation of a naval quarantine issued by the President identified clearly that action by the Soviet government was called for. Although international institutions and a formal proclamation were used, the finger could have been and was pointed with equal explicitness by nonlegal documents, such as the President's letter to Chairman Khrushchev.

There were essentially three substantive demands: the stopping of shipment of offensive weapons to Cuba, the removal of such weapons already there, and verification. The law as such played little role in the formulation of these demands, except that the demands were limited to those on which the United States had the strongest ground. Like a judicial decree, the requests were for no more relief than that to which the action complained of would entitle the United States. The requested relief was not to eliminate Communism from the Western Hemisphere, to oust Castro, to stop all shipments to Cuba, or even to stop all shipments of arms to Cuba. It was narrowly limited to stopping shipments of offensive weapons at a designated point on the high seas and to remove forty-two missiles and other offensive weapons from Cuba.

The political demands with respect to "offensive" weapons might well have profited if language closer to legal precision had been used. The ambiguity in the concept of "offensive" weapons caused the United States some difficulty by permitting the Soviet Union to argue that their missiles were in Cuba for defensive purposes only and that there had been no deception. The Kennedy-Khrushchev letter of October 27 clarified the demand by stating that the first thing that needed to be done was "for all weapons systems in Cuba *capable of offensive use* to be rendered inoperable"* (italics mine).

Governments will typically postpone a decision unless there is some good reason not to. The United States forced a decision with respect to the ships going toward Cuba by establishing the quarantine as of a precise moment, with sufficient advance notice to allow the ship captains time to receive orders from Moscow. The legal concept of signing a proclamation at one time to come into effect at another served well to give the Soviet Union both time for a decision and the necessity of a decision. The deadline for the decision to withdraw the missiles already in Cuba was less clear and was set wholly by nonlegal methods. Apparently Robert Kennedy explained orally to the Soviet ambassador on Saturday, October 27, that time was running out and that the United States was ready to begin military action

---

* T. Sorensen, *Kennedy* (New York: Harper & Row, 1965), p. 714.

by the first of the next week.† There was no deadline for the desired decision to accept appropriate UN inspection, and such a decision was never made.

A major way in which law operates as a tool to help one government influence another is in making more legitimate what is being asked. Legality is not simply window dressing; it can be crucial to success.

The essential demand of the United States—that the Soviet Union not have nuclear missiles in Cuba—was converted by the OAS vote from the purely political demand of a nuclear adversary to the unanimous request of twenty countries of the Western Hemisphere, acting through formal procedures and pursuant to a pre-existing treaty. Countries such as Mexico and Brazil, which had demonstrated their independence of the United States, supported the resolution. The existence of the Rio Treaty and the Organization of American States made it possible to strengthen and make more reasonable the United States demand in this way.

Robert Kennedy regarded this vote as crucial:

It was the vote of the Organization of American States that gave a legal basis for the quarantine. Their willingness to follow the leadership of the United States was a heavy and unexpected blow to Khrushchev. It had a major psychological and practical effect on the Russians and changed our position from that of an outlaw acting in violation of international law into a country acting in accordance with twenty allies legally protecting their position.*

Taking the case to the Security Council of the United Nations also operated to strengthen the legitimacy of the

† E. Abel, *The Missile Crisis* (Philadelphia: J. B. Lippincott, 1966), p. 199.

* *McCall's*, November, 1968, p. 172.

United States position. Going as a plaintiff to the United Nations rather than as a defendant tended to make the United States position appear more defensible.

The particular demand with respect to the quarantine and the stopping of ships was undoubtedly strengthened by having it done with proper care to legalities. A formal proclamation was used, and it was issued only after the vote of the Organization of American States.

Abel reports that Ambassador Llewellyn Thompson "made the point that the Russians were impressed by legalities" and that "If, for example, the Organization of American States should pass a resolution endorsing the blockade, Moscow might be inclined to take it seriously" (p. 87).

Making the quarantine as legal and legitimate as possible was important not only for its direct effect on the Russians. The more legitimate the quarantine appeared to third states, the greater would be the indirect effect of their views on the Soviet Union.

The demand for international inspection of Cuba was never supported by a good—or even plausible—legal case. American insistence on inspection was supported by a Soviet promise, but the Soviet Union clearly had no legal right to invite international inspectors to Cuba. The OAS case against the Soviet Union, demanding the removal of the missiles, was not an equally good case for Cuba's permitting international inspection.

One fear of the United States was that the Soviet Union could, if its planes had a stop en route, fly nuclear warheads to Cuba. The United States relied on international law (and the consequent high cost to the Soviet Union of violating it) to block this contingency. The Soviet Union had a month before requested landing rights in Guinea for a once-a-week flight from Moscow to Havana. The United

States asked the President of Guinea to refuse the Russian request, and he agreed to do so (Abel, p. 137). It was assumed that if it were illegal for the Russians to land at Conakry, they would not do so; if it were legal, they might. Similar action was taken by the United States with respect to the legality of Soviet aircraft landing at Dakar in Senegal (Abel, pp. 136, 137). The implicit American demand that the Soviet Union not fly warheads into Cuba was thus made extremely legitimate. The Soviet Union could not fly warheads without violating the law.

By making offers and threats more legitimate, the law not only made them more acceptable; it also made them more credible. The United States supported each of its three demands with a separate threat. The demand that Soviet ships stop was supported by the threat of shooting them (and the consequent risk of escalation) if they did not. The demand that the missiles be removed was supported by the threat of an air strike or an invasion (and the risk of escalation) if the missiles were not removed. The demand for international inspection was supported by the threat of continued unilateral aerial reconnaissance (and perhaps more) if such inspection was not established. The stronger the United States legal case, the more credible each of these threats, and the less costly it would have been to the United States to carry them out. The international procedures followed and the legal rhetoric advanced in support of the United States position thus operated to make the threats more influential.

Law provided an international mechanism. The fact that the Organization of American States and the United Nations existed made it possible for them to be used to make more legitimate the demands of the United States. But neither organization was in a position to take on the job itself. There

was no inter-American naval force which could take on the
quarantine function. If there had been one, it certainly
would have been used.

There was also no international observation team in existence which could have taken on the verification function.
Kennedy interpreted Khrushchev's letter as a proposal to
remove weapon systems from Cuba "under appropriate
United Nations observation and supervision." Kennedy
also wanted "the establishment of adequate arrangements
through the United Nations to ensure the carrying out and
continuation of these commitments" before the United
States removed the quarantine and gave the desired no-
invasion pledge (Abel, p. 198). There was no established
international machinery for carrying on these functions, and
it proved impossible to create such machinery at the time.
The world was lucky that this fact did not upset the resolution of the crisis.

Despite Khrushchev's assertion that for the United States
Navy to stop Soviet ships on the high seas would be "piracy," it did not look like piracy to the Soviet Union or
to anybody else. The formal proclamation, the designated
zones, the limited list of what would be stopped—in short,
the "legalistic" aspects of what was being done—were tools
used by the United States better to accomplish its task.

An exchange of promises was used as the means for settling the crisis. Although both sides were ultimately interested in what was done rather than what was said, the
Soviet Union decided that it would adopt as an intermediate
goal a formal pledge from the United States not to invade
Cuba. The United States was interested in the physical
removal of weapons but found that in the first instance it
should settle for the exchange of promises—an informal
legal arrangement.

The effectiveness of an action often depends upon its legality. In discussing the quarantine, Sorensen reports:

> We could not even be certain that the blockade route was open to us. Without obtaining a two-thirds vote in the OAS —which appeared dubious at best—allies and neutrals as well as adversaries might well regard it as an illegal blockade, in violation of the UN Charter and international law. If so, they might feel free to defy it [p. 687].

It was on October 22 that President Kennedy announced that "All ships of any kind bound for Cuba from whatever nation or port will, if found to contain cargoes of offensive weapons, be turned back." Nevertheless, recognizing that the effectiveness of the quarantine might depend upon its legality, Kennedy held up the signing of the formal proclamation until after the Organization of American States had authorized it. Abel writes:

> The President was fully prepared to act alone if necessary. But he understood the importance of holding back the proclamation until the OAS had voted. It was, therefore, not until seven o'clock [October 23rd] that the President signed the proclamation, basing the blockade squarely on the unanimous OAS vote invoking Articles 6 and 8 of the Rio Treaty of Reciprocal Assistance [p. 135].

Sorensen has reported the fear that illegality might make the quarantine ineffective:

> . . . Llewellyn Thompson . . . had emphasized the fundamental importance of obtaining OAS endorsement of the quarantine. . . . Thompson's interest was the added legal justification such endorsement would give to the quarantine under international and maritime law as well as the UN Charter. That was important, he said, not only to our mari-

time allies but to legalistic-minded decision-makers in the Kremlin [p. 706].

Law thus operates as a restraint by making certain courses of action, if illegal, either ineffective or counterproductive. That illegality operates as a restraint is the obverse of the fact that legality may serve as a tool.

International law may also operate as a restraint by raising the political cost which a country pays for engaging in certain conduct. There can be little doubt that one of the considerations which restrained the United States from an immediate air strike against the missile sites in Cuba was the gross illegality of such action. The Attorney General is reported to have compared such a surprise attack with Pearl Harbor and stated, "My brother is not going to be the Tojo of the 1960's" (Abel, p. 64). The legal consideration, of course, was not operating independently of general considerations of what is right and what is wrong, or of the facts that an air strike could not be sure to be 100 per cent effective and would result in killing a number of people, including Russians. Abel reports that ". . . it began to appear that the blockade advocates might prevail. Legalities had less to do with this than the practical argument that a naval blockade would avoid killing Russians and give the Kremlin time to reflect" (p. 73).

There was a good argument that even the blockade was a violation of international law. The Soviet Union tried to raise the cost to the United States of its quarantine (as well as to accomplish other objectives) by charging it with piracy and "unheard of violation of international law" (Abel, pp. 127–128). The reputation of the United States as a law-abiding country was no doubt somewhat damaged by the conclusions of Indian newspapers in New Delhi, Bombay, and Calcutta that in blockading Cuba the United States was "violating international law" (Abel, p. 145).

The illegality of engaging in U-2 overflights also, apparently, had operated to reduce the number of flights made and to restrict discussion of them. The United States was undoubtedly concerned, at least in part, with the political cost it would suffer for being found to be acting contrary to international law.

Law also operates as a restraint by raising for each country the fear of setting a harmful precedent. This kind of cost is one that governments often minimize. At least they fail to take it into account to the extent that many international lawyers would like. Abel quotes Dean Acheson as taking "the position that legal niceties were so much pompous foolishness in a situation where the essential security of the United States, its prestige, its pledged word to defend the Americas, was threatened" (p. 72).

For the United States to act unilaterally to the extent that it did could not help but set precedents for unilateral action in the future. One modest way in which fears of damage to the international system did restrain the United States is described by Abel:

Abram Chayes, the State Department legal adviser, suggested a language change. Instead of basing the blockade on Article 51 of the United Nations Charter, which assures each nation's inherent right of self-defense in case of armed attack, Chayes argued that its legal basis should be the right of the OAS to take collective measures in guarding the security of the Americas. To an international lawyer, the distinction had its importance in avoiding the establishment of a self-defense precedent the Russians might use in the future (Abel, p. 115).

Probably the decision not to engage in an immediate air strike on Cuba reflected concern not only for the reputation of the United States but also for the impact which such lawlessness might have on the future of international relations.

The decisions consciously taken during the Cuban missile crisis were ones in immediate pursuit of the substantive objective of removing missiles from Cuba. The various roles which international law played in the decision process of the United States government is not fully appreciated without considering some of the decisions which had previously been made by default—decisions which had not been made because questions were not raised. There are a limitless number of "might-have-beens" which are suggested by the missile crisis. One way to appreciate them is to ask these questions: What rules of substantive international law and what changes in international machinery would the United States have liked to have had on hand when the missile crisis started? Why was it that the United States had decided not to press for these substantive rules and this international machinery?

The United States would have been in a stronger position if some international conduct to which it was going to object as violently as it did to the Soviet introduction of missiles into Cuba had been not merely objectionable but also illegal. Prior action by the United States designed to improve the international system might have been able to bring the legal rules into closer conformity with the rules which the United States intended to "enforce." This might have been done through the establishment of a Latin American nuclear-free zone, through OAS action outlawing non–Western Hemisphere military bases in the Western Hemisphere, or perhaps through agreement between the Soviet

Union and the United States regarding the deployment of missiles. Such an agreement might have been possible in August, 1962, when President Kennedy first decided to withdraw United States nuclear missiles from Turkey (Abel, p. 191).

The United States might have been better off if the United Nations had had in existence a small stand-by inspection staff, with standard operating practices that the Cuban government could have been asked to accept. Rather than being confronted with the task of working out new arrangements acceptable to the Soviet Union, United States, Cuba, and the United Nations, there would have been a greater chance of international inspection if some such facility had been in existence. The United States had previously "decided" (perhaps by ignoring the possibility) not to press for the establishment of such an international inspection staff.

The Cuban missile crisis suggests that in appraising the role of international law in government decision making we should look not only at its role in the decisions which consciously were made but also at its role in decisions which were made by default.

8

As It Looks to the
Hard-Working Bureaucrat

THE foregoing chapters argue that it would make sense for a government to look at international affairs in terms of such a rational analysis. The United States could be more effective if the government focused attention on decisions they wanted another government to make and ran through an organized check list of what might be changed to make those decisions more likely. Why doesn't this happen?

People in the government usually have two answers: "These ideas are entirely too theoretical," and "We go through that kind of analysis already." In a sense, both are true. The limited role which reasoned analysis of a problem can play becomes explicable when we step inside the government and look at what goes on. Machiavelli was advising a single prince, a man who could make a governmental decision all by himself. Today a governmental decision is the product of a vast bureaucracy which, in turn, is democratically responsible to a large constituency. If we do not like the decisions that come out, we must look at the machinery which produces them.

A hypothetical account of a single decision will put a little flesh, if only make-believe, onto the organizational skeleton which determines how a foreign policy decision is formulated. Let us assume that a deputy assistant secretary in the Office of International Security Affairs in the Department of Defense has just received a copy of a cable from Lisbon reporting that fighting has broken out in Angola, that Portugal is sending in reinforcements, and that some African countries are talking about intervening in Angola to help end colonialism.

One course of action would be for him to sit down and carefully formulate possible decisions which the United States might seek from Portugal, the rebel leaders in Angola, and the various African states. He might work out as best he could how the pros and cons of each of those decisions probably look to the people concerned at the moment, and then consider how those pros and cons might be altered to make more likely those decisions we would like the various parties to make. He could then work out proposed actions by the United States which would appropriately structure the choices open to the governments concerned and convincingly communicate those choices to them. He could prepare the operational documents required to produce these actions by the United States government. Finally, he could prepare his written analysis of the alternatives and of their comparative costs, risks, and benefits to the United States.

It would take a great deal of effort for this official to work up such papers. But it is not laziness which causes him to avoid such theoretical analysis. If he were to start on this task, others in the United States government would have reacted to the incoming news long before he came up with his results. His study would be by-passed by events. His work would probably have no impact on the action taken. Furthermore, it is not his job to consider all aspects of American foreign policy relating to the Angolan crisis: he is to focus on military matters. Others are to be concerned with African affairs, with our relations with Portugal, with our information program, with our actions in the United Nations, and so forth. Those problems are not the task of our deputy assistant secretary.

He starts at the other end and begins to work on a cable to Lisbon. He knows that the first man with a draft has an advantage. As he works on the draft a number of considerations are in his mind: If the cable can be worded so that it is simply an application of a prior decision or a prior statement by the President or another high official, the cable will be more difficult for others to object to, it can be cleared at a low level, and it can be dispatched more quickly. He looks through his loose-leaf notebook of presidential and other quotations relating to armed intervention, wars of independence, and colonialism. At the same time, he is thinking about what his immediate superior, the assistant secretary, would want him to come up with. After all, a deputy is supposed to produce a draft his boss would want to recommend to the Secretary, or be able to justify if it should go out without the Secretary's clearance.

A deputy assistant knows that there will be a meeting on this cable among those in the different offices and departments involved. He does not want this meeting to become bogged down in big and unanswerable questions. If his cable involves anything that is new or controversial, it is likely to meet opposition. Experience has taught him that a short cable that is covered by prior policy statements wins more support than a cable that breaks new ground. A bright idea is, almost by definition, inconsistent with prior government policy. It is likely to get shot down by a consensus of those present at the meeting. Worse than that, the deputy's reputation and effectiveness within the government will be weakened if he advances an idea that is rejected. Too many failures and he will become known as someone who is unrealistic—as someone to whose views one need not pay much attention. His future in the government depends upon his having a low failure rate. Before he comes up with anything original, he will want to see which way the wind is blowing.

While this deputy is working on a draft cable, half a dozen other people in the government are thinking about the Angolan problem and are also thinking about what it is that they should suggest. They are reviewing past governmental statements on Africa, intervention, and the role of the United Nations in such uprisings. Each of them is also thinking about the kind of proposal which could be cleared throughout the government with the least difficulty and delay.

At the meeting on the cable the discussion will be practical. The immediate question will be what the United States should do or say in response to the situation in Angola. It is not surprising that agreement tends to settle upon the lowest common denominator. There is no need to reach agreement on reasons if those present can reach agreement on the immediate action to be taken.

The outcome of the meeting is likely to be a cable to Lisbon, with copies to other embassies, asking that the respective governments be reminded that the United States has always been in favor of self-determination but is opposed to the settlement of such questions by bloodshed and violence, that the United States is willing to work with others in bringing about a peaceful resolution of the problem, and believes that this should be accomplished within the framework of the United Nations. United States ambassadors will also be asked to make sure that the governments concerned appreciate the dangers of intervention and the risks inherent in the situation. There will also be no objection from other departments to the State Department's proposed release stating that the United States government is concerned over developments in Angola, that officers have been instructed to follow the situation closely, and that the President is being kept fully informed.

Such a decision may not be the wisest one for the United States government to make. It tends to be the easiest and hence the most probable. It does not focus on the task of influencing what other countries do. It does not focus on their decisional problems but on our own. Such a cable is the product of domestic institutions and it reflects the concerns of the men who staff these institutions. The case of the deputy assistant suggests some of these concerns. Three general features of the way governments work help to explain why good people usually produce inadequate decisions:

1. *Subordinate officers act as deputy judges, not advocates.* If the government is to act wisely, they should consider not only the most probable decisions but also some that at the outset appear unpromising. In looking for what to do, the net should be cast widely and the cases in favor of a number of quite different suggestions developed. In a court of law the adversary process is used to make sure that positions which may not at first appear to have much

merit are fully explored. The lawyer who is defending an accused man is not asked to recommend a decision or to advance a view that he thinks has a high chance of being adopted, but rather to advance to the judge the case for deciding the matter one way. He is advancing a point of view. He is presenting considerations which ought to be taken into account—and weighed against others—in reaching a decision. The arguments in favor of one course of action are fully explored and clearly articulated before becoming watered down by offsetting considerations. This adversary process tends to assure that the institution as a whole gives full consideration to the possibilities.

The role of a government officer who suggests a course of action to his superior is quite different. To be sure, there is within the government a great deal of controversy and a great deal of advocacy. By and large, however, it is like an argument among judges, not among counsel. Each official is supposed to take everything into account. The junior staff officer in the State Department or in the Defense Department in recommending action with respect to the bombing of North Vietnam is expected to make a "realistic" recommendation which takes into account the political costs on the Hill which the President may encounter in making one decision or another. Domestic political considerations are considered at every level. The President is rarely given the chance to hear what someone thinks "ought" to be done if only domestic considerations would permit. The man who advises the President about what ought to be done and the man who advises the adviser are expected themselves to take into account the domestic considerations and make a realistic proposal.

The State Department man is not expected to recommend an end of the bombing of North Vietnam unless he believes that such a decision is politically feasible. The President, finding that even his foreign policy advisers do not recommend an end of the bombing, is reluctant to end the bombing. The foreign-aid adviser is supposed to recommend the appropriations that can realistically be expected. Each man from the bottom up adjusts his expert view to take adequate account of political realities. It is no wonder that the domestic political climate weighs heavily in the final decision.

2. *The premium placed on success tends to minimize effectiveness.* There are substantial personal costs to a government official in pushing ideas which are rejected. It might occur to a State Department official that the United States ought unilaterally to drop some of its restrictions on travel and trade with Cuba. He might think that this would increase the strength of United States influence within Cuba or that it would demonstrate American flexibility. What would happen if that idea were to be advanced but not adopted? One possible treatment of this outcome by his superiors would be favorable commendation. They might thank him for raising the point, assure him that the government could not know that they were pursuing the wisest possible course except by comparing it with alternative policies, explain their reasons for rejecting the idea, and urge him to continue to re-examine policies and suggest new ideas no matter how unlikely their adoption seemed.

Such comments are possible, but experience suggests that they are not common. The officer is likely to be told that his suggestion was contrary to the existing policy, and he may be made to feel that making the suggestion showed poor judgment. Perhaps a public statement would be issued to deny that the government was giving any consideration to removing restrictions on trade or travel with Cuba. This might be accompanied by a further statement that all responsible officials of the government were in support of the government's policy.

The White House issued such a statement following publication in December, 1962, in the *Saturday Evening Post* of the "charge" that Adlai Stevenson had suggested during the Cuban missile crisis that the United States might withdraw its missiles from Turkey in exchange for the withdrawal of Soviet missiles from Cuba. It would have been grossly irresponsible of our officials if that idea had not been advanced within the government and throughly canvassed. The President had decided several months before that our nuclear missiles should be withdrawn from Turkey. If the Soviet missiles could be withdrawn from Cuba in exchange for something we had decided to do anyway, the risks of war might be reduced at no practical cost to the United States. Whether or not the idea should have been adopted, it should have been advanced and considered. Mr. Stevenson felt compelled to deny that he had ever made the suggestion, and the White House issued a statement that Mr. Stevenson "strongly supported" the President's decision.

Such statements bring home to a government officer that it is poor strategy to make suggestions which are not adopted. In rare cases an officer may be asked to play the devil's advocate, but otherwise he had better be on the side of the angels; it is in his interest to be identified after the event as having been on the side which favored the policy that was adopted. As of any one day, an existing policy is more likely to be continued than changed. The safest bet is to be opposed to change.

As J. D. Williams wrote in 1957: ". . . any critic can establish a wonderful batting average by just rejecting every new idea." This method of achieving a high degree of success is widespread (but not universal) within the government. It produces a general reduction in the effectiveness of government officers. An officer may start off with a high expectation of getting things done. It is almost always more difficult to get decisions through the governmental bureaucracy than the inexperienced man believes. A number of projects fail. The officer becomes more realistic. He is able to reduce his failure rate: he reduces the number of his ideas which are shot down by reducing the number proposed. So "improvement" is accomplished by reducing the number of things he tries to do—by reducing the amount of change he seeks to bring about. The less he tries to do, the less he gets done. A schematic graph of a man's first two years in government might look something like this:

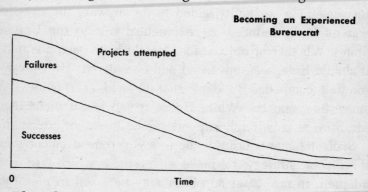

Becoming an Experienced Bureaucrat

Projects attempted

Failures

Successes

0   Time

This chart summarizes the bureaucratic life of a New Dealer, a Kennedy appointee, or almost any idealistic young man who joins the foreign service. With the passage of time he becomes more realistic, more practical. He stops advancing "half-baked" ideas. He becomes more careful in the ideas he advances. Most of those he now advances are adopted. But he is getting less than half as much done as he was when he started.

3. *Decisions expand with time.* A third institutional feature which causes a government to act irrationally is the

undue weight which governments often give to prior decisions.

It is impossible at the time a decision is made to distinguish precisely between what has been decided and what has not. Governments often *try* to define the scope of what has been decided. Sometimes there is an attempt to make the decision big—a decision of "policy." In 1932, for example, Secretary of State Stimson declared that the United States "does not intend to recognize any situation, treaty, or agreement which may be brought about by means contrary to the covenants and obligations of the Pact of Paris of August 27, 1928. . . ." The decision was defined to apply to a large category of cases and for a long period of time. On other occasions the attempt is to define the scope of the decision narrowly. The decision of the United States to provide compensation to the Japanese fishermen who were injured by fall-out from nuclear tests in the Pacific was intended to be a "one-shot" decision applying only to that particular situation. The statement accompanying the compensation said it was being tendered *"ex gratia . . . without reference to the question of legal liability."*

Despite what may be said at the time a decision is made, however, the effective scope of what has been decided cannot be defined at that time. That scope is determined by subsequent actions of the government. Situations will necessarily arise which involve facts not thought of or not fully appreciated at the time the first decision was made. People will then have to decide whether or not the first decision affects what should now be done. Even the explicit statement that a decision shall not be a precedent cannot eliminate its effect as a precedent. At the least, it has set a precedent for accompanying decisions with the statement that they are not a precedent. A government, like a maiden, cannot avoid the future impact of a decision to yield by asserting that what is in fact a precedent shall not be deemed a precedent.

There is a degree to which a decision ought, as a rational matter, to govern future conduct. As long as the facts and the perceived choices are substantially the same, then a decision by the same or a higher level of government ought, presumptively, to be followed. As a general rule, there is no reason to expect that a fresh decision in such a case will be any wiser than the first. There are positive costs in diverting intellectual resources from other problems to the reconsideration of a solution already devised in a similar situation. Further, there are administrative advantages in consistency. The task for the person faced with a subsequent choice in such a case is to determine whether the facts and choices are so similar to those considered at the time of the first decision that the differences do not justify re-examining the problem.

It is irrational for a government to give prior decisions either greater or less scope than they deserve. Governments tend to give too much scope to precedent. Conclusions reached on one set of facts are applied to different facts. Conclusions reached on limited information continue to be followed even after much more information is available— information which could be expected to lead to a different decision. Conclusions reached in haste are followed even though there is now time to think through the matter more carefully. There are a number of reasons for this harmful practice.

Although consistency is a virtue, it is deemed by officials to be even more of a virtue than it is. This is a result of a government's concentrating their attention in foreign affairs on their own decisions rather than on the decisions of other governments. If we think of actions in the field of foreign affairs as announcements of our policy and the making of our decisions, then changes in policy or the reversal of decisions suggests that mistakes have been made. If we recognize, however, that in foreign affairs the important decisions are those of other governments and that our actions are best considered as attempts to influence them, consistency becomes less of a virtue. Persistence in pursuing an unsuccessful means of exerting influence is certainly not presumptively the wisest course of action. And in the United States consistency of approach over time is what officials believe the public wants. New ideas are all right so long as they are not inconsistent with old ones.

Another reason inducing officers to treat a past decision as if it preclude examination of a situation which involves facts and considerations not previously weighed is the administrative ease of doing so. It is far simpler to treat a matter as one governed by a prior decision than to treat it as a new problem. Every day new matters come up. The preliminary question confronting an officer is to decide whether or not the matter is governed by the prior decision. One might guess that of all the situations in which this preliminary question is raised, about half would be found to be covered by the prior decision and half would not. The incentive for the officer to resolve the preliminary question one way rather than the other, however, is strong. If he decides that this matter is governed by the prior decision, his work is done. Time is saved, the problem is dealt with, and he can go on to other things. If, however, the officer decides that the problem is essentially a new one, not governed by a prior decision, he has taken on a lot of work, not only for himself but for others as well. They must develop the alternatives, examine the pros and cons, and reach bureaucratic agreement on what should be done. Faced with such disparate consequences it is not surprising that, unconsciously if not consciously, the preliminary question is usually resolved in favor of treating the matter as governed by prior decision.

The limited authority of each officer further operates to cause past decisions to grow with time. A subordinate official has authority to implement prior decisions but not to restrict them by making other decisions of equal importance. A junior officer can treat past decisions as applying to present circumstances despite the passage of time and the appearance of facts not previously considered. A presidential decision not to trade with Castro's Cuba was reached under certain factual conditions. The decision was presumably not to trade with Cuba for the time being. Without further authority lower officials of the government can apply that decision to factual circumstances different from those considered by the President. They can also extend indefinitely the period of time for which trade shall be cut off. They can probably even tighten the implementation of the decision so that it applies to trade through third states. Lower officials do not, however, have authority to impose a limit to the original decision to block trade. Even if they believe that the factual situation has so changed that the reasons underlying the prior decision are no longer applicable, they cannot on their own authority say that the decision is no longer controlling. They cannot say that a reasonable time has now passed and that trade can be resumed. Only the President can cut off the continuing effect of his prior decision. Lower officers can expand the decision. It is possible for them to apply it to unexpected circumstances and to future conditions far different from those weighed and contemplated at the time of the original

decision. It is not surprising that, with this one-way authority, decisions tend to grow with time and to be applied to facts and circumstances radically different from those originally taken into account. Although the President is free to say that his prior decision is no longer applicable, he is unlikely to do so unless that question is put on the agenda and brought to his attention with staff recommendations. It is usually an uphill fight for any staff man to try to do so.

The following of a prior decision has a cumulative effect. Precedent builds upon precedent. Each time a prior decision is treated as applying to somewhat different facts, there is now a precedent which itself will be applied to facts still further removed from these originally considered. This is particularly true in the case of policies designed to extend into the future. The decision not to trade with Cuba is extended one day after the next. The gradual change in facts from yesterday to today will rarely seem sufficient to justify drawing an end to the original decision and re-examining the matter afresh.

In government decisions as in the law, the dead hand of the past thus governs more than it should. A decision to take a step in a particular direction becomes a decision to pursue that course indefinitely until major and obvious considerations require some shift.

9

What Can an Outsider Do?

THIS book may appear to be a criticism of how officials conduct our foreign policy. It may also appear to be a criticism of how our government is set up to pursue international objectives. The real target of my criticism, however, is the critics. In my judgment, the responsible critics of government are drastically falling down on their job. Newspapers, magazines, commentators, and elected political figures regularly demand the wrong kind of performance from the official concerned with foreign affairs. They ask him to play to the grandstand, not to get results. They themselves judge performance not by international results but by the short-term effect on popularity.

Prime Minister Wilson's policy toward Rhodesia following that country's unilateral declaration of independence was dominated not by considerations of how to get a reasonably good result for the majority of the Rhodesian population but rather by considerations of how to maintain and strengthen the Labour Party majority in the House of Commons. Moves taken were not designed to influence white Rhodesian leaders to make a decision Britain wanted them to make. They were designed to influence politicians in Britain to continue to support Harold Wilson. In the United States, recognition of China is essentially an issue of domestic politics. It is responsive to its probable effect on the Gallup Poll, not its probable effect on China.

In a democracy this is the way things are. It is perhaps the way they should be. If the public wants athletes who play to the grandstand, that is the kind to which we are entitled. If we want wrestling to be a staged performance rather than the best of wrestling skill, that is what we will get. If the qualities of an automobile upon which we insist are flashy chromium trim, maximum horsepower, and a soft ride, we can expect an automobile that is unsafe at any speed. If the qualities of a foreign policy upon which we insist are flashy public statements, maximum military power, and little consideration of the specific decisions we would like others to make, we can expect a foreign policy that is also unsafe at any speed.

It is as easy to blame the State Department for its product as it is to blame General Motors for theirs. And each must assume some responsibility. The major fault, however, lies in those outsiders who affect the demand. Where the situation is personal and close at hand, we often realize that performance is more important than public relations. One gets suspicious of the doctor who is cultivating the parent rather than concentrating his attention on the sick child. If we insist that a public-school teacher adhere to politically unobjectionable clichés, we should not expect him to have much originality or perhaps much success in stimulating his students. A town which demands that its mayor spend his time making speeches and greeting visitors pays a high price in terms of the jobs that do not get done. We do not ask a mechanic for consistent policy statements of his attitude toward different makes of automobiles. We want him to diagnose the difficulty and get to work on it. And when the mechanic does so, he is not ignoring his constituency. He is being responsive to public demand. It is simply that in these cases the public is more enlightened.

Still one more analogy—an extended one—may be useful. The leaders of a country can be compared with a bus driver proceeding along a dangerous road, the passengers being the public whom the driver must continue to please if he is to retain effective control over the bus. If the only way that he can please the passengers is to drive with his eyes on them, noting their smiles and their frowns and trying to meet the passengers' demand for personal attention, the bus is in danger. Alternatively, the passengers can demand that the driver keep his eyes on the road. Instead of talking to the driver about his popularity on the bus, they can ask him where he thinks he is going and how he proposes to get there. In either case the driver is responding to the will of his public, as he must. It is the public—and its most vociferous and responsible voices—which determines whether the external affairs of the bus are conducted by someone with both eyes in the rear-view mirror or by someone with his eyes on the road.

Even when most of the passengers do care more about the way the bus is being driven and where they are going than they do about personal attention from the bus driver, the way in which they seek to influence the driver often directs his attention to the internal problems of the bus, not the external ones. If they want the bus to be driven more carefully with greater attention to where it is going and how it is going to get there, they may threaten to revolt or to vote for another bus driver, or begin throwing rocks through the windows. Some other technique for influencing the driver, however, may be more successful. They might make some specific suggestion about what turn to make at a future intersection in the road and seek to convince the driver that the passengers would truly be more content to have him keep his eyes on the road than to worry about them.

It turns out that influencing our own government is like influencing another government. The ideas spelled out in this book are as applicable to the man who is in conflict with his government as they are to the government which is in conflict with another. The natural tendency of the critic is to attack actions of the past and to threaten punishment. Such a threat may be to refuse to serve in the government, to vote against them, or to organize a third party. Important as such threats may be, they may not be the best way to exert influence. The very critics of United States policy in Vietnam who argued that militant threats were a poor and ineffective way to influence political leaders tried to influence the political leaders of the United States by militant threats. Just as Hanoi is most easily influenced if it is confronted with a decidable choice that is politically acceptable, so, too, the United States government is most easily influenced if they are confronted with a decidable choice that is politically acceptable.

What applies to particular choices in foreign affairs applies also to the entire approach to foreign affairs. Those critics who are dissatisfied with a State Department which devotes too much attention to attitudes and platitudes should work out some specific decisions which the United States government might realistically be expected to make

—decisions which would change the institution for the better.

Senators and congressmen constitute one identifiable group of critics of our foreign-policy apparatus. It may be useful to look at the kind of influence they can exert upon the government, since they in turn are responsive to all of us. It is often said that elected officials can have little constructive impact on foreign affairs which are so dramatically in the hands of the Executive branch. In the rapidly moving international field, legislative action is often too little and too late. The Senate gives more consent than it does advice.

On particular day-to-day decisions the dominance of the Executive is clear. But on the general problem of increasing the rational content of our foreign policy, Congress is in an ideal position. It can regularly ask the State Department what decisions it wants other governments to make and how it proposes to cause such decisions to be more likely. It can ask the government to establish regular procedures for thinking about such questions.

To be specific, let me suggest the following as a rough draft of a letter from the Senate Foreign Relations Committee to the Secretary of State:

DRAFT

Dear Mr. Secretary:

The Foreign Relations Committee has decided to undertake a general review of the current objectives of the United States with respect to other governments and of the means being pursued to accomplish those objectives. For these purposes we have thought it might be useful to identify many of our objectives in terms of specific decisions which we would like other governments to make. To enable our staff to prepare for hearings would you be so kind as to ask each desk officer concerned with a particular country to prepare a working paper which covers the following points:

1. *Current objectives (decisions)*. A list of specific decisions which, in his view, we would like the government concerned to make (or not to make) and which we could realistically expect that they might make (a) within the next year and (b) within the next two or three years. This should be limited to questions which are sufficiently open and of sufficient interest to the United States government to justify our trying to exert influence. Where several quite different decisions would be equally satisfactory to the United States, it would still be desirable, if only for illustration, to suggest one or more specific decisions which we would welcome.

2. *Current objectives (other)*. Some of our objectives abroad cannot be formulated in terms of the action or inaction which we would like from other governments but rather in terms of results which we hope to bring about by our own actions, or in terms of changes in attitudes. Perhaps there are other categories as well. These should be listed as other specific objectives of United States foreign policy within the country concerned.

3. *Possible additional objectives*. Here should be listed potential decisions by the government concerned or other potential objectives which for one reason or another have not been currently identified as objectives of the United States but which merit consideration or about which there is or would be reasonable doubt or difference of view.

4. *The pros and cons as seen by the other government of making the decisions we desire*. For each of our objectives —each of those decisions we would like another government to make—the working paper should set out our best estimate of the consequences of making the decision as they probably appear to the government concerned and the consequences of their not making it.

5. *Current measures*. The paper should list measures currently being undertaken by the United States for the purpose of influencing the government concerned or for the purpose of attaining some other objective of the United States. This

list should include a brief explanation of why each objective has not already been attained and of how the United States expects to attain its objectives by pursuing these measures.

6. *Possible additional measures.* The paper should also list potential actions and programs of the United States which for one reason or another are not currently being pursued but which merit consideration or about which there would be reasonable doubt or difference of view.

For activities of the United States government which are directed toward an international organization or where we may be trying to influence persons other than a government, working papers along comparable lines should be prepared.

The Committee recognizes that it is asking for specificity where, in many cases, it does not exist. The Committee also recognizes that there is no magic to be accomplished by requesting the preparation of still further paper work. We do, however, think that it might prove useful to examine much of our foreign policy not as centrally concerned with decisions by the United States government but rather as centrally concerned with decisions which will be made by other governments—decisions which we may have some power to influence but which we cannot make for them.

Much of the value of these working papers as tools to aid us all in our thinking would be lost if an attempt were made to reconcile them with each other and to produce polished and internally consistent policy statements. Under these circumstances and to avoid unnecessary editing and revising, would you ask each desk officer to send a copy of his working paper in draft form directly to Mr. _____ of the Committee staff. These drafts will be considered as administratively confidential and, of course, as subject to revision at any time without embarrassment.

SINCERELY YOURS,
CHAIRMAN, SENATE FOREIGN
RELATIONS COMMITTEE

Even more important than such a broad-brush approach to our foreign policy is that pointed questions be asked at the time particular issues are being discussed. Whether the topic is trade with China or trade with Rhodesia, apartheid or DeGaulle, colonialism or nonproliferation of nuclear weapons, some questions are more likely to play a constructive role than others. Today, perhaps, the most frequent questions run something like this:

What happened?
Whose fault was it?
What do you think is going to happen?
Why?
Do you agree with what we are doing?

A set of questions more likely to stimulate rational action in the future might run something like this:

What would we like to have happen next?

Whose decision can bring that about?

What kind of decision could we realistically expect them to make?

Why haven't they made such a decision already?

What might we do to make such a decision more likely?

What alternative courses of action ought to be considered?

What are the costs and risks of trying to affect their decision?

Today reason plays a small role in international affairs. Perhaps ten per cent of international decisions reflect a purely rational judgment of what ought to be done. Enormous pressures and limitations close in upon those who must make the decision. Our task, I suggest, is to see that the role of reason, however small, is well played. And, if we are given the time, reason may well earn for itself a larger role.

Addendum

An Example

WHILE this book was in gestation, some of its ideas were being tried out in actual international conflicts. At one time, I thought of doing this book by applying the approach to a single international dispute, showing how different techniques would apply as the situation developed chronologically. But the successive drafts, memoranda, and notes on just one ongoing conflict would themselves fill a book. And the chances are that the analytical framework that was in my mind would have been all but swallowed up by discussions of substance and by material reflecting competing perceptions of how diplomacy ought to be conducted. So here, in an addendum, is a sample package aimed at getting one limited but significant yesable proposition before an appropriate decider.

With respect to such an example, one particular perception of diplomacy deserves comment. In considering whether or not to undertake a given diplomatic initiative, one naturally tries to estimate its chance of success. By my standards, one chance in a hundred may be good odds indeed. If an individual exerting only part time effort for a week has a slight chance of hastening the end of a war, reducing tension in an inherently dangerous conflict, or directing governmental attention to more constructive pursuits, then his effort is a good investment. It might be compared with drilling an oil well for a few thousand dollars where there is a slight chance of making millions, or with getting a particular sweepstakes ticket for a dollar where there is one chance in a hundred of its winning a fortune. In such circumstances, the question is not "Will my modest investment be wasted?" but rather "Is there a better investment? Is there anything I can do that is more promising, considering the low cost and the possibility of high return?" Government officials tend to apply a different standard, at least as to action that may become public. Here they are reluctant to try anything which is "probably" going to fail. To a given official, the cost of doing nothing is slight; the cost of trying and failing is likely to seem higher. Rarely is it enough to convince him that he knows of no alternative which holds greater promise and that failure would not work any appreciable damage. He will measure the plan, regardless of its low cost, against a 50-50 standard: unless it is more likely than not to succeed, he will be disinclined to try.

This point is relevant to the following pages, which are intended to illustrate the approach suggested in this book. After the book had gone to press, I devoted a couple of days to thinking about the Middle East and produced the following memorandum and attached drafts. If an outside government or some UN official wanted to apply the thinking of this book to the Middle East, these drafts suggest a starting point. They try to present such an activist with a yesable proposition making it easy for him in turn to present similar ones to the United Arab Republic (U.A.R.) and to Israel, the parties which hold the key to progress in the Middle East. These suggestions might be considered the first move in the application of theory to a given case with which most people are pretty familiar.

I have no illusions that these suggestions provide "the answer" to the Middle East or that they will probably work. Certainly the approach presently being pursued by the United States and most other governments is "not working" either, by any objective standard of performance. The papers below simply suggest an approach which if pursued with sustained effort might have a better than one in a hundred chance of bringing about significant improvements in the Middle East situation. I know of no more promising approach to suggest to third parties who are more interested in reducing the level of conflict in the Middle East than in seeing one party or another "win"—that is, to those who are more interested in peace and justice than in victory.

MEMORANDUM

March, 1969

To:
From: Roger Fisher
Re: Middle East

You encouraged me to put on paper some of my thoughts on the Middle East. Here they are in the form of a memorandum and some operational drafts. It is not my thought that these drafts eliminate the necessity of negotiation. Rather they provide a focus for it.

Certainly there is not going to be a single comprehensive settlement of the Middle East, a "Versailles Treaty" signed by all the governments involved which provides us with a once-and-for-all solution to the problems of Suez, the Strait of Tiran, the Jordan River, demilitarized zones in the Sinai, the Gaza Strip, Israel's boundaries, the Golan Heights, repatriation and resettlement of refugees, recognition, diplomatic relations, Jerusalem and the holy places, Transjordan, compensation problems, and the United Nations observers and forces.

The Security Council's unanimous Resolution 242 of November 22, 1967, lays down the provisions and principles for peace in the Middle East, namely:

withdrawal of Israeli forces from territories occupied in the June, 1967, war;
termination of all claims or states of belligerency;
acknowledgment of the right of every state in the area to live in peace;
respect for secure and recognized boundaries;
freedom of navigation through international waterways in the area;
a just settlement of the refugee problem;
demilitarized zones and other guarantees of territorial inviolability.

We should, I believe, accept this resolution as providing an adequate framework for settlement. I see no chance of getting anything better.

Within this context we should concentrate first on the most easily decidable questions. I would start with the United Arab Republic and Israel and seek to obtain from each the best decision which one might reasonably expect to obtain at this time. I would then go on, step by step and piece by piece, first identifying in each case an actual document such as a declaration, an offer, a promise, an invitation, a letter or a request which would be helpful and which one might be able to obtain, and then trying to get it.

As an agenda, I suggest the following:

1. Privately review the attached drafts yourself and consult informally with others who are fully aware of the political sensitivities of the governments concerned.

2. Prepare clean drafts reflecting suggested improvements.

3. Arrange a meeting with President Nasser. The objective of this meeting would be to obtain from him the best obtainable letter addressed to the Secretary General. Oral discussion would obviously be desirable to convey the proper balance between yesability and flexibility. The first set of attached documents is for such a discussion. These documents are:

I. Draft Aide Memoire to be left with President Nasser after the meeting. This summarizes the points which would be made orally and identifies the various working papers used in the discussion, namely:

A. The Way Israel May See Its Choice Today

B. Draft Letter from President Nasser to the Secretary General designed to change the choice facing Israel

C. The Way Israel Might Be Persuaded to See Its Choice Later (Target Situation)

D. The Costs and Benefits to the U.A.R. of Sending the Letter

4. Without waiting for a letter from President Nasser it may be desirable to proceed independently and concurrently with the Prime Minister of Israel, and confront his government with a decidable question in the form of a letter which they might be expected to sign. If you are unable to obtain any letter from the U.A.R. you should certainly try Israel.

5. A second set of documents should be prepared for such discussions. Attached, marked II-B, is a draft of a proposed letter from Israel to the Secretary General, prepared on the assumption that no prior letter has been obtained from the U.A.R. The other documents are not included here but could be drafted on the same principles as those for the U.A.R. The full set would be:

II. Draft Aide Memoire to be left with the Israeli Prime Minister after the first meeting. This is comparable to the one prepared for President Nasser. It would summarize the major points which would be made orally and identify the various working papers used in the discussion, namely:

A. The Way the U.A.R. May See Its Choice Today

B. Draft Letter from Israel to the Secretary General designed to change the choice facing the U.A.R.

C. The Way the U.A.R. Might be Persuaded to See Its Choice Later (Target Situation)

D. The Costs and Benefits to Israel of Sending Such a Letter.

6. Further steps would have to be planned in the light of the results of the foregoing, yet work should be done now on drafts which would help identify potential yesable propositions, such as:

—a letter from Jordan to the Secretary General regarding Transjordan.

—a draft of a General Assembly resolution on Jerusalem.

—a draft deed of internationalization of the Strait of Tiran.

—a draft letter from Israel to the Secretary General regarding refugees.

Draft No. 1

AIDE MEMOIRE

Ambassador ———— met with President Nasser of the United Arab Republic in Cairo on ————, 1969, to discuss the present impasse in relations between Israel and the Arab countries and to propose, in the light of the position presently being taken by the Government of Israel, certain initiatives by the United Arab Republic designed to obtain withdrawal of Israeli forces from U.A.R. territory and progress toward implementation of Security Council Resolution 242 of November 22, 1967. The Ambassador made the following points:

1. It is unlikely that the United Arab Republic will be able in the foreseeable future to establish through forces of arms a durable and satisfactory solution to the problems of the Middle East. No physically imposed solution appears promising. Improvement in the situation will require political decisions of governments, including in particular the Government of Israel.

2. It is unlikely that a complete political settlement can be effected all at once. The number of parties and the complexity of the issues involved appear to preclude a comprehensive document settling all questions and signed by everyone. It would appear to be to the interest of the U.A.R. to focus attention on one issue at a time and attempt to exert influence upon Israel to make a desired decision with respect to that issue. It is far easier to gain international political support behind a clear, simple step than in support of complicated multilateral measures.

3. One step with which the settlement process could begin would appear to be a partial withdrawal of Israeli forces from the Sinai combined with an opening of the Suez Canal. It is suggested that an effort be made to bring this about.

4. Draft A (attached) suggests the way the withdrawal question may now look to the Government of Israel. If this draft is even approximately correct it is not surprising that Israel has declined to start the withdrawal of its troops. The

task for the U.A.R. is to do what it can on the political side to so change the choice with which Israel is faced that withdrawal can reasonably be expected. This will require making it politically easy for Israel to withdraw and politically difficult for them not to. It will require demonstrating to the major powers and other third parties that the U.A.R. has adopted a reasonable position—has in fact done all that it can reasonably be asked to do at this stage—and that therefore it is up to Israel to take the next step.

5. An appropriate initiative for the U.A.R. to consider is a letter to the Secretary General of the United Nations along the lines of Draft B (attached). Such a letter would keep the United Nations directly involved. It should not be limited to making proposals but should be an operative letter which in itself constitutes action. This will suggest to everybody that it is up to Israel to do something next.

6. The draft letter involves no great change in position for the U.A.R. except that of playing some cards now rather than holding them to be played later. To bring political pressure to bear on Israel it is necessary for the U.A.R. to undercut Israel's statements about Arab objectives and to state clearly an Arab position that is in fact reasonable and will also appear reasonable to all but the most ardent Zionists.

7. For the U.A.R. to send such a letter would confront Israel with a new choice which would look something like that outlined in Draft C (attached). In these circumstances it might reasonably be anticipated that Israeli withrawal of its forces would begin, that the existing stalemate will have been broken, and that further measures regarding refugees, the establishment of demilitarized zones, and the completion of withdrawal could more easily be undertaken.

8. While the proposed initiative involves some risks and some costs to the U.A.R., these appear to be less than those involved in allowing the present situation to continue. A rough estimate of the choice with which the U.A.R. is now faced is reflected in the balance sheet shown in Draft D (attached). Although a decision could be postponed, the passage of time

is likely to cause increased international acceptance of Israel's occupation of U.A.R. territory as a permanent feature.

9. Should President Nasser send a letter along the lines of the attached draft, efforts would be undertaken by others to persuade Israel to make a constructive response.

Draft A

THE WAY THE CHOICE MAY NOW LOOK TO ISRAEL

The Decision: Shall we start to withdraw troops now before the Arabs accept Israel, proper boundaries, and demilitarized zones —and if so how and when?

The consequences if we do

(+) We please the Arabs and foreign doves.

BUT:

(—) We have to figure out how and when to do what.

We give up the gains of the '67 war.

We go back to wholly unacceptable conditions.

We subject ourselves to heavy domestic criticism.

We rely on the United Nations which has not protected us in the past and has in fact condemned us.

We let Suez be cleared with no guarantee that our ships can go through.

The consequences if we don't

(—) We subject ourselves to some foreign criticism.

BUT:

(+) We hold defendable boundaries.

We continue to strengthen our hand in the occupied areas.

We have strong domestic support.

We rely on our own arms which have defended us so well.

We make sure that if Suez is opened we will be able to use it.

His Excellency U Thant
Secretary General
United Nations
New York, New York

Dear Mr. Secretary General:

More than a year of discussions regarding the implementation of the Security Council's Resolution 242 of November 22, 1967, has demonstrated the unlikelihood of the parties themselves reaching agreement on a single, comprehensive document covering all aspects of the implementation of that resolution. Even if agreement on such a document could be reached, one could expect disagreement in turn over its implementation. We believe that the implementation of the decision of the Security Council need not await further formal acceptance or agreement but should be undertaken at once by the United Nations, and should proceed concurrently on all parts of the Resolution.

The United Arab Republic has been blamed by Israel for delay in the restoration of peace in the area. We, in turn, find that the fault lies on the side of Israel. You know the strong resentment we feel over the injustices of the past. You are fully aware of the double standard which condones organized attacks by the Israeli Government against its neighbors and condemns Arab citizens for resisting the illegal occupation of their own countries.

But the time has come to look forward, not back. To facilitate the work of the United Nations in the implementation of Security Council Resolution 242 we make this formal statement:

1. The United Arab Republic accepts the General Assembly resolution of 1947 establishing a new state in the Middle East, accepts the fact that that state exists, that it is a member of the United Nations, that like its neighbors it is entitled to all the rights and protections and is subject to all the obligations

of states provided in the Charter of the United Nations, and that that state is called Israel.

2. The United Arab Republic accepts the fact that the international boundaries of Israel are no more restrictive than those provided in the 1949 Armistice Agreement and no more extensive than those of the territory occupied by Israeli forces as of June 4, 1967. The exact location of the final boundaries between these positions is a matter to be settled peacefully through the United Nations. It is a matter as to which the United Arab Republic does not claim the right to use force.

3. As a demonstration of our earnest desire to move forward even before Israeli troops have been fully withdrawn from our territory, we hereby commit ourselves to allow cargo to and from Israel to pass through the Suez Canal as soon as all Israeli troops have withdrawn at least 40 km. from the Canal and the Canal can be opened.

4. We understand that Israel wants the Canal to be open not only to cargoes going to and from Israel but also to vessels flying the Israeli flag. So long as Israel is engaged in the belligerent occupation of U.A.R. territory we regard it as unduly provocative to have ships flying its flag pass through our territory. Nevertheless, to avoid any doubt that the Canal shall in the future be open to Israeli flag vessels, the United Arab Republic hereby authorizes you to declare the formal end of belligerency between the U.A.R. and Israel whenever you or your successor as Secretary General are satisfied that the military occupation of our territory has ceased and that the other provisions of Security Council Resolution 242, including those relating to refugees, are in the process of being fully implemented. We hereby accept the fact that when the state of belligerency has ended as described above both Israeli cargoes and Israeli flag vessels shall thereafter have the right to pass as freely through the Suez Canal and through the Strait of Tiran and the Gulf of Aqaba as do the ships of any other nation.

5. The United Arab Republic is willing to agree that a portion of its territory along the Israeli border shall remain demilitarized and subject to the presence of United Nations

personnel, placed there pursuant to Security Council or General Assembly authorization, who shall not be subject to removal except by UN decision provided that on the Israeli side of the boundary as well there are fair and reasonable demilitarized zones subject to the same terms.

6. We suggest that you establish an advisory committee over which you preside, assisted by Ambassador Jarring or another representative chosen by you, to work out proposals regarding refugees, demilitarized zones, international waterways, withdrawal of troops, guarantees and so forth to be submitted to the Security Council in the implementation of Resolution 242. The Permanent Representative of the United Arab Republic to the United Nations is prepared to meet at any reasonable time and place with you or your representative together with anyone, including a diplomatic representative of the State of Israel, whom you or your representative may wish to invite to discuss any matter you may wish to have discussed.

To lessen the risk of future misunderstanding let me make our position clear. We accept as a physical fact the geographical existence of the State of Israel and, when it gets back within the borders it was respecting two years ago, we will not use force against it. We are not, however, prepared to recognize politically the present Government of Israel as a legitimate government, whether judged by its domestic or its international behavior. We are also not prepared—certainly not at this time—to establish direct diplomatic relations with the Government of Israel, nor are we prepared to engage in any bilateral meeting or ceremony which appears to accord our approval of that government or of its policies.

After the history of Israel's imposition into the Middle East it is enough to ask Arab states to accept the political fact that the State of Israel exists. It is too much to ask Arab states to put a stamp of approval upon a government which officially discriminates against non-Jews. One would have thought that Jews, who have put up with so much discrimination over the years, would be the last people on earth to make Jewishness again a basis for governmental discrimination. The discrimination of the Israeli Government against Arabs is based on grounds just as immoral and just as illegitimate as any discrimination by South Africa against blacks or by pre-war Germany against Jews. The fact that Hitler's discrimination was against Jews and that Israel's discrimination is in favor of Jews and against Arabs is not a distinction which appeals to Arabs. To ask Arabs to "accept" the Government of Israel as it is today is like asking Jews to "accept" the Government of Germany as it was thirty years ago. Today countless refugees are prevented from returning to their homes and their land on one ground only—they are not Jews. They cry out in their misery for help.

Zionist Israel is today a Frankenstein creature, unwilling to abide by international law or the unanimous decisions of the Security Council of the United Nations. The Government of Israel insists that it may decide as it likes what is right and what is wrong; that it may freely inflict military punishment wheresoever it likes upon whomsoever it likes, for whatever reason seems sufficient to it alone.

We will continue by every peaceful means to work toward the day when Israel will become a modern political state in which all of its citizens, regardless of their race or religion, may freely participate without discrimination. We will work for the day when Israel will respect the standards of decent international behavior, when it will honor its firm commitment to the United Nations to refrain from force or threats of force and to accept the decisions of the Security Council. When that day comes there will be no problem of good relations among the countries of the Middle East.

This letter is written as one step toward that day. We request, as a second step, that the United Nations, through Security Council action if necessary, decide that Israeli troops should promptly withdraw a distance of 40 km. or more from the Suez Canal and that the Canal be opened to all ships that went through it before, but that in addition cargoes to or from Israel should be allowed to pass through the Canal.

I hope you regard this statement as constructive and that it will enable the United Nations to proceed more promptly with the implementation of Resolution 242.

Please accept, etc.

Draft C

THE WAY ISRAEL MIGHT BE PERSUADED TO SEE ITS CHOICE LATER
(Target Situation)

The Decision: The U.A.R. letter having been sent and published, shall we, Israel, withdraw our troops 40 km. from the Suez Canal?

The consequences if we do

(+) We start a process which may bring peace and security to the Middle East.

The Canal will be re-opened and cargoes to and from Israel will be able to go through.

We have face-to-face discussions with the U.A.R., but only under UN auspices.

We make the U.A.R.'s acceptance of the state of Israel and the 1967 boundaries more binding.

We still hold substantial U.A.R. territory as leverage.

We can always block the Canal again later if we want.

BUT:

(—) We will receive criticism from our own military and other hard liners.

It is not certain when and if Israeli flag vessels will be able to use the Canal.

The consequences if we don't

(—) The present pattern of terror and reprisals is likely to continue and get worse.

The Canal remains blocked.

The Arabs will not talk with us, nor will third parties press them for bilateral talks.

We risk losing such acceptance of Israel as the U.A.R. has given.

We will receive heavy criticism from abroad and even from some citizens.

The U.S. Government may stop sales of military equipment and even consider other measures.

There is little chance of bringing international pressure to bear on Arabs to make further concessions.

BUT:

(+) We retain control over all of the Sinai and continue to block the Canal.

Draft D   I-D

THE COSTS AND BENEFITS TO THE U.A.R. OF SENDING THE LETTER

The Decision: Shall we, the U.A.R., send a letter to the Secretary General along the lines of the suggested draft?

The consequences if we do

(+) We start a process of Israeli withdrawal from our territory.

The Suez Canal opens and we begin to get revenue from it again.

Foreign criticism of the U.A.R. is reduced.

Foreign political pressure on Israel is increased.

We increase the chance of doing something for the refugees.

BUT:

(—) We receive domestic criticism from some military and other hard liners.

We risk dividing the Arab countries.

We write the letter without knowing for sure what we will get for it.

The consequences if we don't

(—) Israeli occupation of our territory continues.

The Suez Canal remains closed, and we get no revenue from it.

Foreign criticism of the U.A.R. continues.

It will be difficult to get the big powers to exert any pressure on Israel to withdraw.

The plight of the refugees continues.

There is little to look forward to but another war which we may not win.

BUT:

(+) The military support the government.

The Arabs are more or less united against Israel.

We could always write such a letter later.

His Excellency U Thant
Secretary General
United Nations
New York, New York

Dear Mr. Secretary General:

Upon becoming Prime Minister I reviewed our entire position to see if there were not some way in which Israel could help move the Middle East question closer to settlement. Israel continues to be under attack from Arab terrorists whose actions are condoned and often supported by Arab governments. The Arab states continue to refuse to recognize Israel or to meet with us to work out a peaceful future.

As you know, we believe that the solution to the problems of the area should be worked out to the extent possible in direct bilateral discussions. We do not contemplate a master treaty signed by all the countries of the region nor the imposition of some comprehensive United Nations plan. The problem will be more manageable if it is broken up into pieces. This approach should also allow the parties at one discussion more easily to reach a solution to a particular problem on its merits. We are prepared to have such bilateral discussions take place under United Nations auspices. Some problems, such as that of refugees, would undoubtedly require meetings among more than two countries.

To further the possibilities for settlement and to inaugurate this process, Israel makes the following formal statement and proposals with respect to the United Arab Republic.

1. We ask you to seek now from the United Arab Republic a written declaration which will include, in substance, the following language:

The United Arab Republic accepts the right of the State of Israel to exist, the U.A.R. will never use or condone the use of force to affect or harass the existence of Israel within borders as they existed on June 1, 1967, or as they may later be agreed upon, and the U.A.R. recognizes the permanent right of Israeli ships and cargoes to pass through the Suez Canal.

2. As soon as you receive and make public such a declaration on behalf of the Government of the United Arab Republic, Israel will immediately order its military forces to withdraw a distance no less than 40 km. from the Suez Canal and will permit the Canal to be cleared and opened to traffic.

3. To reduce the risk of incidents in the immediate future we hereby assure you that during the first year after the Canal has been opened we will be willing, upon your request, voluntarily to refrain from sailing vessels flying the Israeli flag through the Canal except on a few token or symbolic occasions to demonstrate that their right to pass through the Canal has been accepted.

4. If within the next two months the U.A.R. makes a declaration as provided in paragraph 1, Israel hereby commits itself to the eventual return of all of the Sinai territory to the United Arab Republic, on the condition that a large part of it on the United Arab Republic side of the border constitute a demilitarized zone subject to the presence of United Nations personnel who could not be withdrawn except by agreement, or by decision of the Security Council upon no less than 60 days' notice. And under the same conditions Israel is willing to have United Nations personnel stationed in limited, designated demilitarized zones on its side of the border as well. Special arrangements will have to be made with respect to the area bordering on the Strait of Tiran to assure free passage through that waterway.

5. If within the next two months the U.A.R. makes a declaration as provided in paragraph 1 we further undertake to assist in the task of the resettlement of all refugees who formerly lived in areas now in Israel and agree that some of these shall be allowed to return to Israel if they desire to be repatriated here, and that all others who once lived in what is now Israel will receive at least some compensation, either directly or indirectly, to assist in their resettlement.

6. The Permanent Representative of Israel to the United Nations is prepared to meet with you or your representative

at any reasonable time and place, together with anyone, including a diplomatic representative of the United Arab Republic, to discuss any matter you propose. To facilitate the progress of such talks we suggest that they be private.

We hope that this statement will serve as a constructive basis for beginning a process of settlement which will secure peace in the Middle East.

Please accept, etc.

Index

Index

ABOUT THE AUTHOR

ROGER FISHER is a Professor of Law at Harvard University. His major field is international law. He has concentrated his attention on the relationship between law and governmental conduct, teaching seminars and courses with such names as Legal Method in International Disputes, The Relevance of International Law, Enforcing International Law, and United Nations Law and Problems of World Order.

He is on the Board of Trustees of the Hudson Institute and is a member of the Council on Foreign Relations, of the Executive Council of the American Society of International Law, and of the Commission to Study the Organization of Peace. He is a consultant on international security affairs to the Department of Defense and an associate editor for *The Journal of Conflict Resolution*. He has published a number of articles dealing with arms control, international law and conflict. He is editor and a co-author of the book, *International Conflict and Behavioral Science—The Craigville Papers* (Basic Books, 1964).

Over the past twenty years, while in private practice and while teaching at Harvard, he has advised various foreign governments with respect to international disputes. He has recently been legal adviser to the Government of Anguilla, a small Caribbean island whose international status remains in dispute.